Southern Cornmeal & Grit

Cornbread, Polenta, Casseroles & More!

S. L. Watson

Copyright © 2015 S. L. Watson

All rights reserved.

ISBN: 9781073705269

No part of this book may be reproduced or utilized in any form or by any means, electronic or mechanical, including photocopying and recording without express written permission from the author and/or copyright holder. This book is for informational or entertainment purposes only. Cover design S. L. Watson 2015. Picture courtesy of Canva.

The author has made every effort to ensure the information provided in this book is correct. Failure to follow directions could result in a failed recipe. The author does not assume and hereby disclaim any liability to any party for any loss, damage, illness or disruption caused by errors and omissions, whether such errors and omissions result from negligence, accident or any other cause.

The author has made every effort to provide accurate information in the creation of this book. The author accepts no responsibility and gives no warranty for any damages or loss of any kind that might be incurred by the reader or user due to actions resulting from the use of the information in this book. The user assumes complete responsibility for the use of the information in this book.

DEDICATION

To southern food lover's everywhere!

CONTENTS

	Introduction	i
1	Cornmeal	1
2	Grits	91

INTRODUCTION

Cornmeal is most famous for cornbread and hush puppies. Southern cooks use cornmeal in a variety of recipes. There is no doubt that cornbread is delicious, but hush puppies, bread and grits add double pleasure to your taste buds.

In this cookbook, you will find over 160 recipes for cornbread, hush puppies, polenta, main dishes and grits. Most dishes are quick to fix and you can serve your family a wholesome meal in no time. Cornmeal can be made into a pastry crust for savory pies. A quick sandwich bread can be made from cornmeal.

My family loves polenta. Included are our favorite polenta recipes. Use the basic polenta recipe and add toppings to the polenta you have on hand in the pantry or refrigerator. Fried or baked polenta slices are a wonderful way to clean out the refrigerator. Almost any topping is delicious on them.

Cornmeal and grits make budget friendly casseroles and main dishes. Beans or vegetables served over grits or hot fresh polenta is an economical and tasty way to serve cornmeal and grits.

I bake cornbread specifically to use as a sandwich bread. You make your favorite cornbread batter as usual. Grease a rimmed cookie sheet with grease just as you would grease your pan if making cornbread. Pour a thin layer of batter onto the cookie sheet. Bake for 10-12 minutes or until the cornbread is done and golden brown.

Remove the cookie sheet from the oven. Let the cornbread sit for 5 minutes. Cut the cornbread into squares about the size of a loaf of bread. Use the squares just as you would bread for sandwiches. You can also use a large round cookie cutter and make round sandwiches if preferred.

1 CORNMEAL

Serrano Chile Blue Cornbread

Makes a 10" cast iron skillet

1 1/4 cups blue cornmeal
1 cup all purpose flour
1 tbs. baking powder
1 tsp. salt
1/8 tsp. baking soda
2 tbs. granulated sugar
2 tbs. unsalted butter
3 Serrano chiles, finely chopped
1 green bell pepper, finely chopped
2 tbs. vegetable shortening
2 eggs, beaten
1 cup buttermilk
1/3 cup melted unsalted butter
1/3 cup melted vegetable shortening
2 tbs. sour cream or plain yogurt
11 oz. can white corn, drained
3 tbs. fresh chopped cilantro

In a large mixing bowl, add the blue cornmeal, all purpose flour, baking powder, salt, baking soda and granulated sugar. Whisk until combined. Set the bowl aside for the moment.

In a skillet over medium heat, add 2 tablespoons butter, Serrano chiles and green bell pepper. Saute the peppers for 4 minutes. Remove the skillet from the heat.

Preheat the oven to 450°. Add 2 tablespoons vegetable shortening to a 10" cast iron skillet. Place the skillet in the oven until the shortening melts and the skillet is sizzling hot. This takes about 5 minutes in my stove.

Add the eggs, buttermilk, 1/3 cup melted butter, 1/3 cup melted vegetable shortening, sour cream, corn and cilantro to the skillet with the peppers. Stir until well combined and add to the dry ingredients. Stir only until the batter is combined and moistened. Pour the batter into the hot skillet. Bake for 20-30 minutes or until the cornbread is done in the center and lightly browned. Remove the skillet from the oven and serve hot.

Southern Cornbread

Makes a 10" cast iron skillet

4 tbs. bacon drippings, melted
2 eggs
2 cups buttermilk
2 cups plain white or yellow cornmeal
1 tsp. salt
1 tsp. baking soda
2 tsp. baking powder

Preheat the oven to 475°. Add 2 tablespoons melted bacon drippings to a 10" cast iron skillet. Place the skillet in the oven for 4 minutes or until the skillet and drippings are sizzling hot. While the skillet is heating, add the eggs and buttermilk to a mixing bowl. Whisk until well combined. Add the cornmeal, salt, baking soda, baking powder and 2 tablespoons bacon drippings. Whisk until combined.

Pour the batter into the hot skillet. Bake for 15-20 minutes or until the cornbread is baked in the center and golden brown. Remove the skillet from the oven and serve hot.

Carrot Cornbread

Makes a 9" square pan

1 cup all purpose flour
1 cup yellow or white plain cornmeal
1/4 cup granulated sugar
3 tsp. baking powder
1 tsp. salt
1/4 cup unsalted butter, softened
1 egg, beaten
2 carrots, peeled and shredded
1 cup whole fat buttermilk
1 tbs. vegetable oil or bacon drippings

Preheat the oven to 425°. In a mixing bowl, add the all purpose flour, cornmeal, granulated sugar, baking powder and salt. Whisk until well combined. Add the butter to the dry ingredients. Using a pastry blender, cut the butter into the dry ingredients until you have coarse crumbs.

Stir in the egg, carrots and buttermilk. Mix only until combined. Place the vegetable oil in a 9" square baking pan. Place the pan in the oven for 2 minutes or until the oil is hot. Remove the pan from the oven and spoon the batter into the pan. Bake for 20 minutes or until the top of the cornbread is lightly browned and set. Remove the pan from the oven and cool for 5 minutes before serving.

Sour Cream Cornbread

Makes an 8" skillet

2 tbs. vegetable shortening
3 eggs, beaten
1 cup self rising cornmeal
1 cup cream style corn
1 cup sour cream
1/4 cup vegetable oil

Add the vegetable shortening to an 8" cast iron skillet. Preheat the oven to 400°. Place the skillet in the oven for 4 minutes or until the shortening is hot and sizzling.

While the shortening is melting, make the batter. In a mixing bowl, add the eggs, cornmeal, corn, sour cream and vegetable oil. Mix only until the batter is combined and moistened. Pour the batter into the hot skillet. Bake for 18-20 minutes or until the cornbread is baked in the center and golden brown. Remove the skillet from the oven and serve hot.

Honey Cornbread

Makes a 9" square baking pan

1 1/2 tbs. vegetable shortening
1 cup all purpose flour
1 cup plain yellow cornmeal
1/4 cup granulated sugar
3 tsp. baking powder
1/2 tsp. salt
2 eggs
1 cup heavy whipping cream
1/4 cup vegetable oil
1/4 cup honey

Do not use a glass baking dish for this recipe. The difference in temperatures may cause the glass to break. Preheat the oven to 400°. Add the vegetable shortening to a 9" square baking dish. Place the dish in the oven until the shortening melts and the pan is sizzling hot.

While the shortening is melting, make the batter. In a mixing bowl, add the all purpose flour, cornmeal, granulated sugar, baking powder and salt. Stir until combined. In a separate bowl, add the eggs, whipping cream, vegetable oil and honey. Whisk until combined and add to the dry ingredients. Mix only until the batter is moistened and combined.

Pour the batter into the hot baking pan. Bake for 20-25 minutes or until the cornbread is baked in the center and golden brown. Remove the cornbread from the oven and serve hot.

Pecan Cornbread

Makes a 9" loaf

1 tbs. vegetable shortening
1 1/2 cups plain yellow cornmeal
1 cup all purpose flour
1 tbs. baking powder
1 tsp. salt
1/4 cup granulated sugar
1 1/2 cups half and half
2 eggs, beaten
3/4 cup unsalted butter, melted
1/2 cup chopped pecans

Preheat the oven to 375°. Grease a 9 x 5 loaf pan with vegetable shortening. Be sure to grease all the corners of the loaf pan or the bread will stick. In a mixing bowl, add the yellow cornmeal, all purpose flour, baking powder, salt and granulated sugar. Whisk until combined.

In a separate bowl, whisk together the half and half, eggs and melted butter. Whisk until well combined and add to the dry ingredients. Add the pecans and mix only until the batter is combined and moistened. Pour the batter into the prepared pan. Bake about 45-50 minutes or until a toothpick inserted in the center of the bread comes out clean and the bread is golden brown. Remove the bread from the oven and immediately remove the bread from the pan. Serve hot.

Spiced Pecan Cornbread

Makes an 8" iron skillet

2 tbs. unsalted butter, melted
1/2 cup all purpose flour
2 tsp. baking powder
1/4 tsp. salt
1/4 cup granulated sugar
1/2 tsp. ground cinnamon
1/4 tsp. ground allspice
1/4 tsp. ground nutmeg
1/2 cup plain white cornmeal
1/2 cup finely chopped pecans
1 egg, beaten
1/2 cup whole milk

Watch your cooking time carefully as this cornbread will not be as thick as a normal size skillet of cornbread. Add 1 tablespoon butter to an 8" cast iron skillet. Preheat the oven to 400°. Place the skillet in the oven until the pan is sizzling hot. When the butter is hot, brush the butter up the sides of the pan.

In a mixing bowl, add the all purpose flour, baking powder, salt, granulated sugar, cinnamon, allspice, nutmeg and cornmeal. Stir until combined. Add the pecans, egg, milk and 1 tablespoon melted butter. Mix until combined and the batter is moistened. Pour the batter into the hot skillet.

Bake for 20-30 minutes or until the cornbread is done in the center and golden brown. Remove the cornbread from the oven and cut into wedges to serve.

Herbed Cornbread

Makes a 9" square baking dish

1/4 cup plus 4 tbs. melted unsalted butter
1 1/4 cups self rising white or yellow cornmeal
3/4 cup self rising flour
1 tsp. granulated sugar
1/2 tsp. dried marjoram
1/2 tsp. dried thyme
1/4 tsp. celery seeds
2 eggs, beaten
1 1/4 cups whole milk

Do not use a glass pan for this recipe. The difference in temperatures may cause the glass to break. Add 2 tablespoons melted butter to a 9" square baking dish. Preheat the oven to 425°. Place the pan in the oven until the butter and the pan are sizzling hot.

While the pan is heating, make the batter. In a mixing bowl, add the cornmeal, self rising flour, granulated sugar, marjoram, thyme and celery seeds. Stir until combined. Add the eggs, milk and 1/4 cup plus 2 tablespoons melted butter. Whisk until the batter is moistened and combined. Spoon the batter into the hot pan.

Bake for 20-25 minutes or until the cornbread is done in the center and golden brown. Remove the cornbread from the oven and serve hot.

Ultimate Cornbread

Makes an 8" square pan or 9" cast iron skillet

2 1/2 cups chopped onion
1/4 cup unsalted butter
1 cup sour cream
1 cup shredded cheddar cheese
1 tbs. plus 2 tsp. vegetable shortening
1 1/2 cups yellow or white self rising cornmeal
2 tbs. granulated sugar
1/4 tsp. dried dill
2 eggs, beaten
8 oz. can cream style corn
1/4 cup whole milk
1/4 cup vegetable oil
Dash of Tabasco sauce

In a skillet over medium heat, add the onion and butter. Saute for 5 minutes. Remove the skillet from the heat and stir in the sour cream and 1/2 cup cheddar cheese. Set the skillet aside for the moment.

Preheat the oven to 400°. Do not use a glass pan for this cornbread. You will be pouring batter into a hot pan and a glass pan may shatter. Add the vegetable shortening to an 8" baking pan. Place the pan in the oven until the shortening is hot and sizzles.

While the shortening is melting, make the cornbread. In a mixing bowl, add the cornmeal, granulated sugar and dill. Stir until combined. Stir in the eggs, corn, milk, vegetable oil and Tabasco sauce. Stir only until blended and pour the batter into the hot pan.

Spread the onion mixture over the top of the batter. I spoon dollops of the onion mixture over the batter and then lightly spread over the top of the batter. Sprinkle the remaining 1/2 cup cheddar cheese over the top. Bake for 25-30 minutes or until the cornbread is done in the center, the crust is crisp and the cheese melted and slightly golden. Remove the cornbread from the oven and serve.

Picante Cornbread

Makes 6 servings

1 cup all purpose flour
3/4 cup plain yellow cornmeal
1 1/2 tsp. baking powder
1/2 tsp. baking soda
1/2 tsp. salt
1 cup whole fat buttermilk
2 eggs
1/3 cup picante sauce
1/4 cup unsalted butter

Preheat the oven to 425°. Place an 8" cast iron skillet in the oven to heat for 5 minutes. In a mixing bowl, add the all purpose flour, cornmeal, baking powder, baking soda and salt. Stir until combined.

Add the buttermilk, eggs and picante sauce. Stir until the batter is combined and moistened. Remove the skillet from the oven and add the butter. Return the skillet to the oven to melt the butter for 1 minute. Pour the batter into the skillet. Bake for 18-20 minutes or until the cornbread is done and golden brown. Remove the cornbread from the oven and serve.

Cottage Cheese Cornbread

Makes 8 servings

2 tbs. vegetable oil
2 cups self rising cornmeal
1/4 cup granulated sugar
1 egg, beaten
1 cup whole fat buttermilk
3/4 cup cottage cheese

Preheat the oven to 450°. Place the vegetable oil in a 10" cast iron skillet. In a mixing bowl, add the cornmeal, granulated sugar, egg, buttermilk and cottage cheese. Whisk until well combined. Let the batter rest while the skillet heats.

Place the skillet in the oven for 3 minutes or until the oil is sizzling hot. Remove the skillet from the oven and pour the batter into the skillet. Bake for 20-25 minutes or until the cornbread is done in the center and golden brown.

Custard Cornbread

Makes an 8" square pan

1-2 tbs. vegetable shortening
1 cup plain yellow cornmeal
1/4 cup all purpose flour
1 tsp. cream of tartar
1/2 tsp. baking soda
1/2 tsp. salt
4 tbs. granulated sugar
1 1/2 cups whole milk
1 egg, beaten

Preheat the oven to 400°. Grease an 8" square baking pan with the vegetable shortening. Grease the pan well or the cornbread will stick.

In a mixing bowl, add the cornmeal, all purpose flour, cream of tartar, baking soda, salt and granulated sugar. Mix until combined. Add the milk and egg. Mix only until the batter is combined and moistened.

Spoon the batter into the prepared pan. Bake for 25-35 minutes or until the cornbread is done in the center and golden brown. This cornbread will be soft and tender. Remove the pan from the oven and serve.

Wampus Bread

Makes about 16 cakes

2 cups plain yellow or white cornmeal
1 cup all purpose flour
1 tbs. baking powder
1 tsp. granulated sugar
1 tsp. salt
1 cup minced onion
1 cup peeled shredded potatoes
1 cup evaporated milk
Vegetable oil for frying

In a mixing bowl, add the cornmeal, all purpose flour, baking powder, granulated sugar and salt. Stir until well combined. Add the onion, potatoes and evaporated milk. Mix until the batter is moistened and combined.

Add vegetable oil to a depth of 1" in a deep skillet over medium high heat. The temperature of the oil needs to be about 375°. You will need to fry the cakes in batches. When the oil is hot, drop the batter, by tablespoonfuls, into the hot oil. Cook about 2 minutes per side or until the bread is done and golden brown. Remove the cakes from the oil and drain on paper towels. Add vegetable oil as needed to cook all the cakes.

Molasses Johnnycake

Makes an 8" square pan

1/4 cup plus 2 tbs. melted vegetable shortening
1 cup all purpose flour
4 tsp. baking powder
1 tsp. salt
1 cup plain yellow cornmeal
1 egg, beaten
1/4 cup molasses
1 cup whole milk

Preheat the oven to 400°. Spoon 2 tablespoons melted shortening into an 8" square pan. Grease the pan well with the shortening. In a mixing bowl, add the all purpose flour, baking powder, salt and cornmeal. Stir until combined.

Add the egg, molasses and milk. Mix only until the batter is moistened and combined. Gently stir in 1/4 cup melted vegetable shortening. Spoon the batter into the prepared pan. Bake for 20-25 minutes or until the bread is done in the center and lightly browned. Remove the bread from the oven and serve hot.

Southwestern Cornbread Cakes

Makes about 18 patties

1/2 cup plus 2 tbs. unsalted butter
2 cups self rising white cornmeal
1 cup all purpose flour
2 tbs. granulated sugar
5 eggs
2 cups buttermilk
4 ears fresh corn
1 1/2 cups diced onion
8 oz. can diced green chiles, drained
1 cup soft white breadcrumbs
1/2 cup chopped fresh cilantro
2 tsp. black pepper
1 tsp. garlic salt
1 tsp. cayenne pepper, optional
1 cup mayonnaise
1/2 cup vegetable oil

Preheat the oven to 425°. Do not use a glass baking dish for this recipe. The difference in temperatures may cause the glass to break. Add 1/2 cup butter to a 9 x 13 baking dish. Place the baking dish in the oven until the butter is melted and hot.

In a mixing bowl, add the cornmeal, all purpose flour, granulated sugar, 2 eggs and buttermilk. Whisk until well combined. Pour the batter into the hot pan. Bake for 25-35 minutes or until the cornbread is done in the center and golden brown. Remove the cornbread from the oven. Let the cornbread cool for 30 minutes.

While the cornbread is cooling, cut the corn from the cob. In a large skillet over medium heat, add 2 tablespoons butter and the onion. Saute for 6 minutes. Stir in the corn and saute for 5 minutes. Remove the skillet from the heat.

When the cornbread is cool, crumble the cornbread into a large bowl. Add the onions and corn, green chiles, breadcrumbs, cilantro, black pepper, garlic salt, 3 eggs, cayenne pepper and mayonnaise. Toss until well combined and the cornbread and breadcrumbs are moistened. Form the mixture into 18 patties.

If the mixture is not firm enough to form a patty, cover the bowl and chill for several hours. When time is short, I make this ahead and chill in the refrigerator until ready to use.

Add 2 tablespoons vegetable oil to a large skillet over medium heat. Place a few patties at a time in the skillet. Fry the patties about 3 minutes on each side or until both sides are golden brown. Remove the patties from the skillet and keep the patties warm while you prepare the remainder of the patties.

Add the remaining vegetable oil as needed to fry the remaining patties. To reheat leftover patties, place them on a baking sheet. Heat the oven to 400° and heat about 8-10 minutes.

Frankfurter Cornmeal Patties

This is an easy patty similar to a corn dog.

Makes 4 servings

2 tsp. salt
3 cups boiling water
3/4 cup plain yellow cornmeal
8 oz. cooked frankfurters, minced
1/4 cup vegetable shortening

In a sauce pan over medium heat, add the salt and boiling water. Make sure the water is boiling before adding the cornmeal. Stir constantly and add the cornmeal. Keep stirring until the cornmeal thickens and bubbles. This takes about 5 minutes on my stove. Remove the pan from the heat and stir in the frankfurters.

On a large baking sheet, drop the batter, by heaping tablespoonfuls, onto the baking sheet. Let the patties sit at room temperature until firm and cold.

When the patties are ready, add the vegetable shortening to a large skillet over medium heat. When the shortening has melted and is hot, add the patties. Cook about 2 minutes per side or until golden brown. You will have to cook the patties in batches. Do not overcrowd the skillet or the patties will be soggy. Add additional vegetable shortening if needed to fry all the patties. Serve hot.

Corn Fritters

Makes 2 dozen

2 1/2 cups self rising yellow or white cornmeal
1/4 tsp. cayenne pepper
1/4 tsp. black pepper
1/4 cup finely chopped onion
2 tbs. finely chopped green bell pepper
2 oz. jar diced red pimentos, drained
1 cup cream style corn
1/2 cup boiling water
Vegetable oil for frying

In a mixing bowl, add the cornmeal, cayenne pepper, black pepper, onion, green bell pepper, pimentos and corn. Stir until slightly combined. Add the boiling water and stir until combined. Let the batter rest undisturbed for 10 minutes.

In a deep skillet over medium high heat, add vegetable oil to a depth of 1/4" in the skillet. When the oil is hot, dip a tablespoon in hot water. Use the tablespoon to pick up the batter. Drop the batter, by tablespoonfuls, into the hot oil. You will have to fry the fritters in batches. If you add too many fritters at one time to the hot oil, the temperature of the oil will drop and the fritters will be greasy. Fry about 1 minute on each side or until the fritters are golden brown and done in the center. Remove the fritters from the skillet and drain on paper towels.

Cowboy Cornbread

Makes a 9" square baking pan

1 tbs. bacon drippings
1 1/2 cups plain white or yellow cornmeal
1/2 cup all purpose flour
1/2 tsp. baking soda
1/2 tsp. salt
2 eggs, beaten
2 tbs. vegetable oil
1 cup whole milk
2 cups shredded sharp cheddar cheese
1 cup cream style corn
1 onion, chopped
12 bacon slices, cooked and crumbled
2 tbs. chopped red pimento

Do not use a glass pan for this recipe. The difference in temperatures may cause the glass to shatter. Preheat the oven to 350°. Add the bacon drippings to a 9" square pan. Place the pan in the oven until the drippings melt and are sizzling hot.

While the pan is heating, make the batter, In a mixing bowl, add the cornmeal, all purpose flour, baking soda and salt. Stir until combined. Stir in the eggs, vegetable oil and milk. Mix only until the batter is moistened and combined.

Gently fold in the cheddar cheese, corn, onion, bacon and red pimento. Pour the batter into the hot pan. Bake for 30-40 minutes or until the cornbread is done in the center and golden brown. Remove the cornbread from the oven and serve.

Cheesy Beef Cornbread

Makes a 10" cast iron skillet

2 tbs. vegetable shortening
1 cup plus 1 tbs. plain yellow cornmeal
8 oz. ground beef
3/4 tsp. salt
1/2 tsp. baking soda
1 cup whole milk
16 oz. can cream style corn
2 eggs, beaten
1/4 cup vegetable oil
2 cups shredded hoop or cheddar cheese
1 onion, finely chopped
2 jalapeño peppers, seeded and chopped

Grease a 10" cast iron skillet with vegetable shortening. Sprinkle 1 tablespoon cornmeal over the shortening. Place the skillet over medium heat. Cook until the cornmeal is lightly browned. This will only take a couple of minutes. Remove the skillet from the heat and set aside.

In a separate skillet over medium heat, add the ground beef. Stir frequently to break the meat into crumbles as it cooks. Cook for 5 minutes or until the ground beef is browned and no longer pink. Remove the skillet from the heat and drain off the excess grease.

Preheat the oven to 350°. In a mixing bowl, add 1 cup cornmeal, salt and baking soda. Stir until combined. Add the milk, corn, eggs and vegetable oil. Mix until well combined. Pour half the batter into the skillet with the toasted cornmeal.

Spoon the ground beef, cheese, onion and jalapeño peppers over the batter. Pour the remaining batter over the ground beef. Bake for 45-55 minutes or until the cornbread is done in the center and golden brown. Remove the pan from the oven and serve.

Gouda Cornbread

Makes a 10" cast iron skillet

2 tbs. bacon drippings
1 cup all purpose flour
1 cup plain yellow cornmeal
1 tbs. baking powder
1 tsp. salt
1 cup whole milk
1 egg
5 oz. Gouda cheese, cut into cubes
1/4 cup finely chopped green onions

Preheat the oven to 375°. Add the bacon drippings to a 10" cast iron skillet. Place the skillet in the oven to heat for 5 minutes. The drippings should be melted and the skillet sizzling hot when ready.

While the skillet is heating, make the batter. In a mixing bowl, add the all purpose flour, cornmeal, baking powder and salt. Stir until combined. Add the milk and egg. Whisk until well combined. Gently fold in the Gouda cheese and green onions.

Pour the batter into the hot skillet. Bake for 20 minutes or until the cornbread is done in the center and golden brown. Remove the cornbread from the oven and serve.

Hot Water Cornbread with Variations

Makes 12 patties

2 cups plain white cornmeal
1/4 tsp. baking powder
1 3/4 tsp. salt
1 tsp. granulated sugar
1/4 cup half and half
1 tbs. vegetable oil
1 to 2 cups boiling water
Vegetable oil for frying

In a mixing bowl, add the cornmeal, baking powder, salt and granulated sugar. Stir until well combined. Stir in the half and half and 1 tablespoon vegetable oil. Stir in 1 cup boiling water. The batter needs to be the consistency of cornmeal mush or grits. Stir in the remaining water as needed to make the right consistency. The consistency should resemble thick but pourable pancake batter.

In a skillet over medium heat, add vegetable oil to a 1/2" depth in the skillet. When the oil is hot and shimmers, pour the batter, by 1/4 cupfuls, into the skillet. Cook about 3 minutes on each side or until the patties are done and golden brown. You will need to cook the patties in batches. Add additional vegetable oil as needed to cook all the cornbread patties. The cornbread patties will be done on the first side when the bottom is golden brown and the bubbles have popped on the top of the patty. You cook the patties similar to cooking pancakes.

Bacon Cheddar: After adding the boiling water, stir in 1/2 cup cooked crumbled bacon and 1 cup shredded sharp cheddar cheese. Cook as directed above.

Ham: After adding the boiling water, stir in 1 cup cooked diced ham. Cook as directed above.

Southwestern: After adding the boiling water, stir in 1 seeded and diced jalapeño pepper, 1 cup shredded Mexican cheese, 1 cup whole kernel corn and 1/4 cup minced fresh cilantro. Cook as directed above.

Sour Cream Cornmeal Muffins

Makes about 15 muffins

3 tbs. vegetable shortening
1 cup plain yellow cornmeal
1 cup all purpose flour
1/3 cup granulated sugar
2 tsp. baking powder
1 tsp. baking soda
3/4 tsp. salt
1 egg, beaten
1 1/4 cups sour cream
1/4 cup vegetable oil

Preheat the oven to 425°. Grease your muffin tin with the vegetable shortening. Be sure to grease the muffin cups well or the muffins will stick. In a mixing bowl, add the yellow cornmeal, all purpose flour, granulated sugar, baking powder, baking soda and salt. Whisk until well combined.

In a separate bowl, add the egg, sour cream and vegetable oil. Whisk until well combined and add to the dry ingredients. Mix only until combined.

Place the muffin tin in the oven. Heat the muffin tin for 2-3 minutes or until the vegetable shortening melts and the pan is sizzling hot. Fill the muffin cups about 2/3 full with the batter. Bake for 15-17 minutes or until the center of the muffins are done and golden brown. Remove the muffin tin from the oven. Let the muffins sit for 2 minutes before removing them from the pan.

Serve hot with butter, maple syrup, jam or just eat them plain.

Apple Corn Muffins

Makes 12 muffins

2/3 cup plain yellow cornmeal
2 tbs. granulated sugar
1 tsp. salt
1 cup warm milk
1 egg, beaten
1 cup all purpose flour
2 tsp. baking powder
2 cups thinly sliced apples, peeled

Preheat the oven to 350°. Spray a 12 cup muffin tin with non stick cooking spray. In a mixing bowl, add the cornmeal, granulated sugar, salt, milk and egg. Mix until combined.

Stir in the all purpose flour and baking powder. Mix only until the batter is combined and moistened. Gently fold in the apples. Spoon the batter into the prepared muffin tin filling the muffin cups about 2/3 full. Bake for 20-30 minutes or until the muffins are done in the center and lightly browned.

Remove the pan from the oven and let the muffins cool for 5 minutes in the pan. Remove the muffins from the pan and serve warm or cold.

Everyday Cornmeal Muffins

Makes 1 dozen

3 tbs. vegetable shortening
1 1/3 cups self rising white cornmeal
1 tbs. granulated sugar
1 egg, beaten
1 1/3 cups buttermilk
1/4 cup melted unsalted butter

Preheat the oven to 425°. Grease a 12 cup muffin tin with vegetable shortening. Grease the muffin cups well or the muffins will stick. Place the muffin tin in the oven until the shortening melts and the pan is sizzling hot. This takes about 4 minutes in my stove.

While the shortening melts, make the batter. In a mixing bowl, add the cornmeal and granulated sugar. Whisk until combined. Add the egg, buttermilk and melted butter. Mix only until the batter is moistened and combined.

Spoon the batter into the hot muffin tin filling the muffin cups about 2/3 full. Bake for 18-20 minutes or until the muffin cups are done in the center and golden brown.

Bisquick Cornbread Muffins

Makes 12 muffins

3 tbs. vegetable shortening or bacon drippings
1 1/2 cups Bisquick
1/2 cup plain yellow or white cornmeal
2 tbs. granulated sugar
2 eggs
2/3 cup whole milk

Grease a 12 cup muffin tin with vegetable shortening. Grease the muffin cups well or the muffins will stick. Place the muffin tin in the oven to melt the shortening and heat the pan. Bake for 3 minutes or until the shortening is melted and sizzling hot.

In a mixing bowl, add the Bisquick, cornmeal and granulated sugar. Stir until combined. Add the eggs and milk. Stir until combined. Spoon the batter into the hot muffin tin filling the muffin cups about 2/3 full. Bake for 20 minutes or until the muffins are done in the center and golden brown. Remove the muffin tin from the oven and cool for 5 minutes before removing the muffins from the pan.

Broccoli Cornbread Muffins

Makes about 20-24 muffins

4 tbs. vegetable shortening or non stick cooking spray
8 1/2 oz. pkg. cornbread mix
10 oz. pkg. frozen chopped broccoli, thawed
1 cup shredded cheddar cheese
1/4 cup chopped onion
2 eggs
1/2 cup melted unsalted butter

Preheat the oven to 325°. Grease two 12 cup muffin tins with vegetable shortening. Grease the muffin cups well or the muffins will stick. Place the pans in the oven to heat and melt the shortening while you make the batter.

In a mixing bowl, add the cornbread mix, broccoli, cheddar cheese and onion. Toss until combined. In a separate bowl, add the eggs and melted butter. Whisk until combined and add to the dry ingredients. Mix only until the batter is moistened and combined.

Spoon the batter into the muffin cups filling them about 2/3 full. Bake for 15-20 minutes or until the cornbread is done and golden brown. Remove the pans from the oven and let the muffins cool for 3 minutes before removing them from the pan.

Tomato Corn Muffins

Makes 12 muffins

1/3 cup plus 2 tbs. vegetable shortening
1/3 cup granulated sugar
1 egg, beaten
1 cup whole milk
1 cup all purpose flour
1/2 tsp. salt
1 tbs. plus 1 tsp. baking powder
1 cup plain yellow or white cornmeal
1/2 cup chopped canned tomatoes, drained

Preheat the oven to 425°. Grease a 12 cup muffin tin with 2 tablespoons vegetable shortening. Grease the muffin cups well or the muffins will stick. Place the muffin tin in the oven until the shortening melts and the pan is sizzling hot.

While the shortening melts, make the batter. In a mixing bowl, add 1/3 cup vegetable shortening and granulated sugar. Whisk until well combined. Add the egg and milk. Whisk until well combined.

Stir in the all purpose flour, salt, baking powder and cornmeal. Mix only until the batter is moistened and combined. Gently fold in the tomatoes. Spoon the batter into the muffin cups filling the cups about 2/3 full. Bake for 20-25 minutes or until the cornbread is done and golden brown. Remove the muffins from the oven and cool for 1 minute in the pan. Remove the muffins from the pan and serve.

Parmesan Corn Muffins

Makes about 15 muffins

3 tbs. vegetable shortening
2 cups white self rising cornmeal
3/4 cup all purpose flour
1/2 cup freshly grated Parmesan cheese
1/4 tsp. cayenne pepper
2 1/2 cups buttermilk
2 eggs
2 tbs. vegetable oil

Preheat the oven to 425°. Grease your muffin tin with vegetable shortening. Grease the muffin cups well or the muffins will stick. Place the muffin tin in the oven until the shortening melts and is sizzling hot.

While the shortening is melting, add the cornmeal, all purpose flour, Parmesan cheese and cayenne pepper to a mixing bowl. Whisk until combined. In a separate bowl, add the buttermilk, eggs and vegetable oil. Whisk until combined and add to the dry ingredients. Mix only until combined.

Spoon the batter into the prepared muffin cups filling them about 2/3 full. Bake about 15 minutes or until the muffins are done in the center and golden brown. Remove the muffins from the oven. Cool the muffins for 5 minutes before removing them from the pan. Serve hot.

Spicy Cornbread Muffins

Makes 12 muffins

2 tbs. vegetable shortening
1 1/2 cups plain yellow cornmeal
1 tsp. baking soda
1 tsp. granulated sugar
1/2 tsp. salt
2 eggs
1/4 cup picante sauce
1/8 tsp. cayenne pepper
1/4 cup vegetable oil
1 cup plain yogurt

Preheat the oven to 425°. Grease a 12 cup muffin tin with vegetable shortening. Grease the muffin cups well or the muffins will stick. Place the tin in the oven until the shortening melts and the pan is sizzling hot.

While the pan is heating, make the batter. In a mixing bowl, add the cornmeal, baking soda, granulated sugar and salt. Whisk until combined. In a separate bowl, add the eggs, picante sauce, cayenne pepper, vegetable oil and yogurt. Whisk until well combined and add to the dry ingredients. Mix only until the batter is moistened and combined.

Spoon the batter into the muffin cups filling them about 2/3 full. Bake for 18-20 minutes or until the muffins are done in the center and golden brown. Remove the muffins from the oven and cool for 5 minutes before serving.

Sour Cream & Corn Cornbread Muffins

Makes 12 muffins

2 tbs. vegetable shortening
1 cup self rising yellow cornmeal
1/2 tsp. salt
1/4 cup vegetable oil
1 cup cream style corn
1 cup sour cream
2 eggs, beaten

Preheat the oven to 400°. Grease a 12 cup muffin tin with vegetable shortening. Grease the muffin cups well or the muffins will stick. Place the muffin tin in the oven until the shortening melts and is sizzling hot.

While the shortening is melting, make the cornbread. In a mixing bowl, add the cornmeal, salt, vegetable oil, corn, sour cream and eggs. Whisk until well combined. Spoon the batter into the hot muffin tin filling the muffin cups about 2/3 full. Bake for 20-25 minutes or until the muffins are done in the center and golden brown. Remove the pan from the oven. Let the muffins rest for 2-3 minutes before removing them from the pan. Serve hot.

Cornmeal Yeast Muffins

Makes 3 dozen

1 pkg. dry yeast
1/4 cup warm water
1 3/4 cups whole milk
1/3 cup granulated sugar
1/4 cup vegetable oil
1/4 cup unsalted butter, softened
1 tsp. salt
2 eggs
1 1/2 cups plain white or yellow cornmeal
5 to 5 1/2 cups all purpose flour
Vegetable cooking spray

Add the yeast and warm water to a large mixing bowl. Let the yeast sit for 5 minutes. In a sauce pan over low heat, add the milk, granulated sugar, vegetable oil and butter. Stir constantly and cook until the butter melts. Remove the pan from the heat and cool the milk to 105°.

Add the cooled milk to the yeast in the mixing bowl. Stir in the salt, eggs, cornmeal and 2 cups all purpose flour. Using a mixer on medium speed, mix until well combined. Stir in enough of the remaining flour to make a soft dough. It may take all the remaining flour or you may use 1/2 cup less or more. The dough needs to well combined and soft but not sticky.

Lightly flour your work surface. Place the dough on the work surface and knead about 8 minutes. The dough should be smooth and elastic. Spray a bowl with non stick cooking spray. Place the dough in the bowl. Turn the dough over so all sides of the dough are coated with the cooking spray. Cover the bowl and let the dough rise in a warm draft free location. The dough needs to rise about 1 hour or until the dough is doubled in size.

When the dough has risen, punch the dough down. Divide the dough into 72 equal pieces. Roll each piece into a ball. Spray muffin cup tins with non stick cooking spray. Place 2 balls, side by side, in each muffin cup. Set the pans in a warm place and let them rise about 45 minutes. The dough should be doubled in size. Preheat the oven to 375°. Bake the muffins for 12-15 minutes or until done and golden brown. Remove the muffins from the oven.

Brush the muffins with melted butter if desired. When the rolls are cool, you can freeze the muffins if desired.

Cheesy Cornbread Muffins

Makes 1 dozen

2 tbs. vegetable shortening
1 cup plain yellow cornmeal
1 cup all purpose flour
1 tbs. baking powder
1/2 tsp. salt
1 egg, beaten
1 cup whole milk
1/2 cup vegetable oil
1/2 cup shredded cheddar cheese
1/4 cup chopped green onions
1/2 tsp. paprika
2 tbs. grated Parmesan cheese

Preheat the oven to 425°. Grease a 12 cup muffin tin with 2 tablespoons vegetable shortening. Place the muffin tin in the oven until the shortening melts and the pan is sizzling hot. While the shortening is melting, make the cornbread muffins. In a mixing bowl, add the cornmeal, all purpose flour, baking powder and salt. Whisk until well blended.

In a separate bowl, stir together the egg, milk and vegetable oil. Whisk until combined and add to the dry ingredients. Mix only until the batter is combined. Gently fold in the cheddar cheese and green onions. Spoon the batter into the prepared pan filling the muffin cups about 2/3 full.

Sprinkle the paprika over the top of the muffins. Sprinkle the Parmesan cheese over the top of the muffins. Bake for 12-15 minutes or until the muffins are done in the center and golden brown. Remove the muffins from the oven and cool for 5 minutes before removing the muffins from the pan.

Corn Oat Muffins

Makes 1 dozen

1 1/4 cups buttermilk
1/2 cup plain yellow cornmeal
1/2 cup old fashioned oats, uncooked
2 eggs
3 tbs. light brown sugar
2 tbs. vegetable oil
1 cup whole wheat flour
1 tsp. baking powder
1/2 tsp. baking soda
1/4 tsp. salt

Spray a 12 cup muffin tin with non stick cooking spray. In a mixing bowl, add the buttermilk, cornmeal and oats. Stir until combined and let the batter sit at room temperature for 1 hour. Stir in the eggs, brown sugar and vegetable oil. Whisk until well combined. Add the whole wheat flour, baking powder, baking soda and salt. Mix only until the batter is moistened and combined. Preheat the oven to 400°.

Spoon the batter into the muffin cups filling them about 2/3 full. Bake for 15-20 minutes or until the muffins tops are done and lightly browned. Remove the muffins from the oven and cool the muffins in the pan for 5 minutes. Remove the muffins from the pan and serve.

Tex Mex Corn Muffins

Makes about 16 muffins

1 1/2 cups plain yellow cornmeal
1/2 tsp. baking soda
1/2 tsp. salt
2 oz. jar diced red pimentos, drained
1 cup shredded cheddar cheese
1/2 cup finely chopped onion
1/4 cup chopped green chiles
1 garlic clove, minced
2 eggs, beaten
1 cup whole milk
1 cup cream style corn

Preheat the oven to 400°. I do not grease my muffin tins for this recipe. I have a non stick muffin tin and it does not stick on this recipe. If you think your muffin tin might stick, lightly spray the muffin cups with non stick cooking spray.

Place your muffin tin in the oven ungreased for 10 minutes. The muffin tin needs to be very hot for this recipe. If you are using non stick cooking spray, spray after the muffin tin has heated. In a mixing bowl, add the cornmeal, baking soda and salt. Whisk until well combined. Stir in the red pimentos, cheddar cheese, onion, green chiles and garlic.

In a separate bowl, whisk together the eggs, milk and corn. Add to the dry ingredients and mix only until combined. Spoon the batter into the hot muffin tin filling the muffin cups about 2/3 full. Bake for 25-30 minutes. The muffins should be done in the center and golden brown. Remove the muffins from the oven and immediately remove the muffins from the pan.

Corn Husk Sunflower Corn Muffins

Makes 1 dozen

2 ears fresh corn in husks
2 tbs. unsalted butter
1/4 cup finely chopped onion
1 cup all purpose flour
1 cup plain yellow cornmeal
2 tbs. granulated sugar
1 1/2 tsp. baking powder
1/2 tsp. baking soda
1 tsp. salt
1 cup buttermilk
1 egg
1/4 cup unsalted butter, melted
1 cup shredded cheddar cheese
4 oz. can diced green chiles, drained
1/4 cup sunflower kernels

Remove the husks from the corn but tear the husk into 1/2" strips. Add hot water to a large baking dish. Place the husks in the baking dish to soak. Soak the corn husks for 20 minutes. You should have 48 strips.

Remove the corn from the cob. In a skillet over medium heat, add 2 tablespoons butter, corn and onion. Stir constantly and cook for 5 minutes or until the corn is tender. Remove the skillet from the heat.

In a mixing bowl, add the all purpose flour, cornmeal, granulated sugar, baking powder, baking soda and salt. Whisk until well combined. Stir in the buttermilk, egg and 1/4 cup melted butter. Stir only until the batter is moistened. Add the cheddar cheese, corn with onion and the green chiles with liquid. Stir until combined.

Preheat the oven to 375°. Spray a 12 cup muffin tin with non stick cooking spray. Drain the water from the corn husks. Arrange 4 corn husk across each muffin cup. The muffins will bake in the corn husk so make sure the muffin cups are covered. Pour the batter into the corn husk in the muffin cups.

Sprinkle the sunflower kernels over the top of each muffin. Bake for 18-20 minutes or until the muffins are done in the center and the corn husk dark brown. Remove the muffins from the oven and serve. Serve the muffins in the husk.

You can omit the husk and grease the muffin cups with vegetable shortening if desired. You can substitute 1 cup whole kernel corn or frozen thawed corn for the fresh corn if desired.

Blue Corn Muffins

Makes 2 dozen

1/2 cup diced red bell pepper
1/2 cup diced yellow bell pepper
1/4 cup diced onion
1 tbs. vegetable oil
1/4 cup plus 2 tbs. unsalted butter, softened
1/2 cup plus 4 tbs. vegetable shortening
1 1/2 cups blue cornmeal
1 cup all purpose flour
1/3 cup granulated sugar
1 tbs. baking powder
1 tsp. salt
2 eggs, beaten
1 cup whole milk
1/2 cup half and half
1 cup diced cooked ham

In a skillet over medium heat, add the red bell pepper, yellow bell pepper, onion and vegetable oil. Saute the vegetables for 5 minutes. Add 1/4 cup butter and 1/2 cup vegetable shortening to the skillet. Cook only until the butter and shortening melt. Remove the skillet from the heat.

Preheat the oven to 350°. Grease two 12 cup muffin tins with 4 tablespoons vegetable shortening. Grease the muffin cups well or the muffins will stick. Place the muffin tins in the oven until the shortening melts and sizzles.

In a mixing bowl, add the blue cornmeal, all purpose flour, granulated sugar, baking powder and salt. Stir until combined. Add the eggs, milk, half and half, 2 tablespoons butter and ham to the skillet with the peppers. Stir until well combined and add to the dry ingredients. Stir until well combined. Spoon the batter into the prepared muffin cups filling them about 2/3 full.

Bake for 20-25 minutes or until the muffins are done in the center. Remove the muffins from the oven and serve hot. Plain yellow or white cornmeal may be substituted for the blue cornmeal if desired.

Southern Cracklin' Cornbread

Makes a 9 x 13 baking pan

2/3 cup bacon drippings
4 cups yellow or white plain cornmeal
2 tsp. baking soda
1 1/2 tsp. salt
4 beaten eggs
4 cups whole fat buttermilk
1 cup cracklings

Preheat the oven to 450°. Do not use a glass pan for this recipe. The difference in temperatures may cause the glass to shatter. Place the bacon drippings in a 9 x 13 baking pan. Place the pan in the oven until the bacon drippings are hot and melted.

In a mixing bowl, add the cornmeal, baking soda and salt. Pour 1/2 of the hot bacon drippings into the mixing bowl. Add the buttermilk and eggs and whisk until combined. Gently fold in the cracklings.

Place the baking pan back in the oven until the bacon drippings begin to sizzle. Remove the pan from the oven and pour the batter in the pan. Bake for 25 minutes or until the cornbread is done in the center and golden brown. Remove the pan from the oven and serve.

Paprika Cornbread

Makes an 8" square pan

4 tbs. melted bacon drippings
1 1/3 cups plain white cornmeal
2/3 cup Bisquick
1 tbs. plus 1 tsp. granulated sugar
1 1/2 tsp. baking powder
1/2 tsp. baking soda
1 tsp. salt
1/4 tsp. black pepper
1 1/2 tsp. paprika
2 eggs, beaten
1 1/2 cups buttermilk

Preheat the oven to 450°. Add 2 tablespoons bacon drippings to an 8" square pan. Place the pan in the oven until the bacon drippings and the pan are sizzling hot.

While the pan is heating, make the batter. In a mixing bowl, add the cornmeal, Bisquick, granulated sugar, baking powder, baking soda, salt, black pepper and paprika. Stir until well combined.

Add the eggs, buttermilk and 2 tablespoons bacon drippings to the bowl. Stir only until the batter is combined and moistened. Spoon the batter into the prepared pan. Bake for 25-30 minutes or until the cornbread is done in the center and golden brown.

Buttermilk Corn Sticks

Makes 15 corn sticks

You can use a muffin pan or cast iron skillet instead of corn stick pan if desired.

3 tbs. vegetable shortening or bacon drippings
1 1/3 cups white or yellow plain cornmeal
1/3 cup all purpose flour
1 tsp. baking powder
1/2 tsp. baking soda
1/2 tsp. salt
1 tbs. granulated sugar
1 cup whole fat buttermilk
1 egg, beaten
2 tbs. melted vegetable shortening

Preheat the oven to 400°. Divide 3 tablespoons vegetable shortening between a 15 count cast iron corn stick pan. Place the corn stick pan in the oven until the shortening melts and is sizzling hot.

While the shortening is melting, prepare the cornbread. In a mixing bowl, add the cornmeal, all purpose flour, baking powder, baking soda, salt and granulated sugar. Stir until well combined.

Add the buttermilk, egg and 2 tablespoons melted vegetable shortening. Whisk until well combined. Remove the hot pan from the oven. Fill the corn stick pan about 2/3 full. Bake for 12-15 minutes or until the cornbread is done and golden brown.

Angel Corn Sticks

Makes about 3 dozen

3 tbs. vegetable shortening
1 1/2 cups plain white or yellow cornmeal
1 cup all purpose flour
1 pkg. active dry yeast
1 tbs. granulated sugar
1 tsp. salt
1 1/2 tsp. baking powder
1/2 tsp. baking soda
2 beaten eggs
2 cups whole fat buttermilk
1/2 cup vegetable oil

You need a cast iron corn stick pan to make the corn sticks. You can use a 12" cast iron skillet if desired. Preheat the oven to 450°. Divide the vegetable shortening between the corn stick pans or add the shortening to a 12" cast iron skillet. Place the pans or skillet in the oven until the shortening melts and is sizzling hot.

In a mixing bowl, add the cornmeal, all purpose flour, yeast, granulated sugar, salt, baking powder and baking soda. Whisk until well combined. Stir in the eggs, buttermilk and vegetable oil. Whisk until well combined. Let the batter rest for 4 minutes. Spoon the batter into the corn stick pan filling each corn stick about 1/2 full. Bake for 12-15 minutes or until the corn sticks are done and golden brown.

To cook the cornbread in a 12" cast iron skillet, add the batter to the hot skillet. Bake about 18-22 minutes or until the cornbread is done in the center and golden brown.

Fresh Corn Cornbread

Makes a 9" square baking pan

1/4 cup plus 2 tbs. melted bacon drippings or vegetable oil
1 cup yellow or white plain cornmeal
1/2 cup all purpose flour
1 tbs. plus 1 tsp. baking powder
1 tbs. granulated sugar
1 tsp. salt
1 cup fresh corn, cut from the cob
1 egg, beaten
1 cup whole fat buttermilk

I like to grill two ears of corn on an outdoor or indoor grill for a change of pace when making this cornbread. You do not have to grill the corn but I think the charred corn adds remarkable flavor.

Do not use a glass pan for this recipe. The temperature differences may cause the glass to shatter. Preheat the oven to 475°. Place 2 tablespoons bacon drippings in a 9" square baking pan. Place the pan in the oven until the drippings are sizzling hot. This takes about 2 minutes on my stove.

In a mixing bowl, add the cornmeal, all purpose flour, baking powder, granulated sugar and salt. Whisk until well combined. Stir in the corn, egg, 1/4 cup melted bacon drippings and buttermilk. Spoon the batter into the hot pan. Bake for 20 minutes or until the cornbread is golden brown and crispy. Remove the cornbread from the oven and serve hot.

Cheddar Cornbread

Makes a 10" cast iron skillet

2 tbs. vegetable shortening or bacon drippings
1 cup plain yellow cornmeal
1 cup all purpose flour
2 tbs. granulated sugar
1 tbs. baking powder
1 tsp. salt
1 cup whole milk
2 eggs, beaten
2 cups shredded cheddar cheese

Add the vegetable shortening to a 10" cast iron skillet. Preheat the oven to 425°. Place the skillet in the oven until the shortening melts and is sizzling hot. In a mixing bowl, add the cornmeal, all purpose flour, granulated sugar, baking powder and salt. Whisk until well combined. In a separate bowl, whisk together the eggs and milk. Add to the dry ingredients. Add the cheddar cheese and mix until the batter is well combined.

Spoon the batter into the hot skillet. Bake for 15-20 minutes or until the cornbread is done in the center and golden brown. Remove the skillet from the oven and serve hot.

Honey Cornbread

Makes a 9 x 13 baking pan

2 tbs. vegetable shortening
2 1/2 cups plain yellow cornmeal
1 cup whole wheat flour
2 1/2 tsp. baking powder
1 tsp. baking soda
1/2 cup granulated sugar
1 tsp. salt
2 1/2 cups buttermilk
2 eggs, beaten
2 tbs. honey

Preheat the oven to 425°. Do not use a glass baking pan for this recipe. The glass may shatter when the batter is added. Add the vegetable shortening to a 9 x 13 baking pan. Place the pan in the oven until the shortening melts and is sizzling hot.

While the shortening is melting, make the cornbread. In a mixing bowl, add the cornmeal, whole wheat flour, baking powder, baking soda, granulated sugar and salt. Whisk until combined.

In a mixing bowl, add the buttermilk, eggs and honey. Whisk until combined and add to the dry ingredients. Whisk until well combined. Spoon the batter into the hot sizzling pan. Bake for 20-25 minutes or until the cornbread is done in the center and golden brown.

Savory Cornbread

Makes 6 corn sticks

1 tbs. vegetable shortening
2 jalapeño peppers, seeded and chopped
2 garlic cloves, minced
1/3 cup vegetable oil
1/2 cup plain yellow cornmeal
1/2 cup all purpose flour
2 tsp. baking powder
3/4 tsp. salt
1 tbs. granulated sugar
1 tbs. chopped fresh cilantro
1 egg, beaten
1/2 cup whole milk

Preheat the oven to 425°. Divide the vegetable shortening between a 6 stick cast iron corn stick pan. Place the pan in the oven until the shortening melts and the pan is sizzling hot.

While the shortening is melting, make the batter. In a mixing bowl, add the jalapeño peppers, garlic, vegetable oil, cornmeal, all purpose flour, baking powder, salt, granulated sugar, cilantro, egg and milk. Whisk until well combined and the batter is moistened.

Spoon the batter into the corn stick pan filling them about 2/3 full. Bake for 15 minutes or until the corn sticks are done and golden brown. Remove the pan from the oven and serve immediately.

Mexican Cornbread

Makes 12 servings

1/3 cup plus 2 tbs. melted bacon drippings
1 cup self rising cornmeal
1/2 tsp. baking soda
1/2 tsp. salt
1/2 tsp. granulated sugar
1 cup whole milk
3 jalapeño peppers, seeded and finely chopped
1/2 cup chopped onion
1 1/2 cups shredded cheddar cheese
1 tsp. garlic powder
1 cup cooked whole kernel corn
1/4 cup chopped red pimento

Preheat the oven to 350°. In a 10" cast iron skillet, add 2 tablespoons bacon drippings. Place the skillet in the oven to heat until the skillet and bacon drippings are sizzling hot.

While the bacon drippings are heating, add the cornmeal, baking soda, salt and granulated sugar to a mixing bowl. Stir until well combined. Add the milk, jalapeño peppers, onion, cheddar cheese, garlic powder, corn, red pimento and 1/3 cup melted bacon drippings. Whisk until well combined.

Remove the skillet from the oven and pour the batter into the hot skillet. Bake for 35-45 minutes or until the cornbread is done in the center and golden brown. Remove the skillet from the oven and serve hot.

Garlic Thyme Cornbread

Makes a 9" cast iron skillet

2 tbs. vegetable shortening
1 1/4 cups plain yellow cornmeal
3/4 cup all purpose flour
1 tbs. granulated sugar
1 tbs. plus 1 tsp. baking powder
3/4 tsp. salt
3/4 tsp. garlic powder
1 tsp. dried thyme
2 eggs, beaten
1 cup whole milk
1/4 cup vegetable oil

Preheat the oven to 425°. Add 2 tablespoons vegetable shortening to a 9" cast iron skillet. Place the skillet in the oven until the shortening melts and the skillet is sizzling hot.

In a mixing bowl, add the yellow cornmeal, all purpose flour, granulated sugar, baking powder, salt, garlic powder and thyme. Whisk until well combined. Add the eggs, milk and vegetable oil. Mix only until the batter is combined and moistened.

Pour the batter into the hot skillet. Bake about 20 minutes or until the cornbread is done in the center and golden brown. Remove the skillet from the oven and serve hot.

Hot Mexican Cornbread

Makes a 10" skillet

2 tbs. vegetable shortening or bacon drippings
1 1/2 cups plain yellow cornmeal
1 tsp. salt
1 tbs. baking powder
2 eggs, beaten
2 tbs. chopped green bell pepper
1 cup sour cream
1 cup cream style corn
1/4 cup vegetable oil
1 tsp. Tabasco sauce
2 jalapeño peppers, chopped
1 cup shredded cheddar cheese

Preheat the oven to 350°. Place the vegetable shortening in a 10" cast iron skillet. Place the skillet in the oven until the shortening melts and sizzles. In a mixing bowl, add the cornmeal, salt and baking powder. Whisk until combined. Add the eggs, green bell pepper, sour cream, corn, vegetable oil, Tabasco sauce and jalapeño peppers. Whisk until well combined.

Spoon half the batter into the hot skillet. Sprinkle the cheddar cheese over the top of the batter. Spoon the remaining batter over the cheese. Bake for 35-40 minutes or until the cornbread is done in the center and golden brown. Remove the skillet from the oven and serve.

Sometimes, this batter bubbles over slightly in the oven. Place a baking pan under the skillet to collect any drippings. I have tried this in a 12" skillet to prevent the batter from bubbling over and it cooks fine. Reduce the time by 10 minutes if using a 12" skillet. The cornbread will be thinner and not as full in the large skillet. .

Spinach Cornbread

Makes an 8" square baking dish

1 tbs. vegetable shortening
10 oz. pkg. frozen chopped spinach, thawed
6 oz. pkg. Mexican cornbread mix
1/2 tsp. salt
1/2 cup unsalted melted butter
3/4 cup cottage cheese
1 cup chopped onion
4 beaten eggs

Preheat the oven to 400°. Place the vegetable shortening in an 8" square pan. Place the pan in the oven until the shortening melts and is sizzling hot. Remove the pan from the oven.

Pat the spinach dry with paper towels to remove all the moisture. In a mixing bowl, add the spinach, cornbread mix, salt, melted butter, cottage cheese, onion and eggs. Mix until well combined. Spoon the batter into the prepared pan.

Bake for 30 minutes or until a toothpick inserted in the center of the cornbread comes out clean and the cornbread is golden brown. Remove the pan from the oven and serve.

Pecan Cornmeal Rounds

Makes 8 rounds

3/4 cup plus 2 tbs. unsalted butter, softened
1 1/2 cups all purpose flour
1/2 cup plain yellow cornmeal
2 tbs. granulated sugar
3/4 tsp. salt
1 egg, beaten
3/4 cup chopped pecans

Add the butter to a mixing bowl. Using a mixer on medium speed, beat until smooth and creamy. This takes about 2 minutes with my mixer. Turn the mixer to low and add the all purpose flour, cornmeal, granulated sugar, salt, egg and pecans. Mix until well blended.

Lay a 12" long sheet of plastic wrap on your work surface. Spoon the dough onto the plastic wrap. Wrap the dough and chill for 1 hour. When the dough is chilled, lightly flour your work surface. Roll the dough out to 1/2" thickness. Using a 3" round biscuit cutter, cut the dough into 8 rounds. Roll the dough scraps again if needed to cut out all the rounds.

Preheat the oven to 350°. Place the rounds on a baking sheet. Bake for 20 minutes or until done in the center and lightly browned. Remove from the oven and serve hot. Use the rounds as biscuits, spoon a cream sauce over the rounds or eat with butter and honey if desired.

Corn Dogs

Makes 10 corn dogs

10 hot dogs
10 wooden skewers, 6" size
1 cup plain yellow cornmeal
1/2 cup all purpose flour
1 1/2 tsp. baking powder
1 tsp. salt
2 tsp. granulated sugar
1/2 tsp. dry mustard
1/4 tsp. black pepper
1/2 cup finely diced onion
1 egg, beaten
3/4 cup whole milk
Vegetable oil for frying

Pat each hot dog dry with paper towels. Stick a skewer in the end of each hot dog. In a mixing bowl, add the cornmeal, all purpose flour, baking powder, salt, granulated sugar, dry mustard, black pepper and onion. Whisk until combined.

Add the egg and milk to the dry ingredients. Mix only until the batter is moistened and combined. The batter will be thick. In a deep fryer or dutch oven, add vegetable oil to a 5" depth in the pot. Heat the oil over medium high heat to 375°. You will have to cook the corn dogs in batches.

While holding the skewer, dip each hot dog in the batter. Let the excess batter drip off the hot dog. While still holding the skewer, place the hot dog in the oil. Let the hot dog cook for 10-15 seconds before dropping the skewer into the oil. Fry about 3 minutes or until the outside is done and well browned. Remove the corn dogs from the oil and drain on paper towels.

Serve with ketchup and mustard if desired.

Corn Dog Bites

Makes 8 servings

1 cup self rising flour
2/3 cup plain white or yellow cornmeal
1 tbs. granulated sugar
2 tbs. vegetable oil
1 egg, beaten
1 cup buttermilk
1 lb. pkg. hot dogs
Vegetable oil for frying

In a mixing bowl, add the self rising flour, cornmeal and granulated sugar. Stir until combined. Add 2 tablespoons vegetable oil, egg and buttermilk. Whisk only until the batter is moistened and combined.

Cut each hot dog into 5 pieces. Pat the hot dogs dry with a paper towel. Dip each hot dog piece into the batter allowing the excess batter to drip off the hot dog. I insert a toothpick into each hot dog piece and use the toothpick as a handle to dip the hot dogs.

In a deep pot or deep fryer, add vegetable oil to a 3" depth. The temperature of the oil should be 375° when ready. You will need to cook the corn dog bites in batches. If you add too many at one time to the hot oil, the temperature of the oil will drop and they will be greasy. Add the corn dog bites to the hot oil. Fry for 1-2 minutes or until the corn dogs are golden brown. Turn the corn dogs over so both sides brown and cook evenly. Remove the corn dogs from the oil and drain on paper towels. Serve with your favorite sauce.

Cornbread Croutons

Makes 2 3/4 cups

1 tbs. vegetable shortening
1/2 cup yellow cornmeal
1/2 cup all purpose flour
1/2 tsp. baking soda
1/4 tsp. salt
1/2 cup buttermilk
2 eggs
2 tbs. melted unsalted butter

Preheat the oven to 450°. Place the vegetable shortening in an 8" square baking pan. Place the pan in the oven until the shortening melts and the pan is sizzling hot.

In a mixing bowl, add the cornmeal, all purpose flour, baking soda and salt. Whisk until combined. Stir in the buttermilk, eggs and 1 tablespoon melted butter. Mix only until the batter is moistened and combined. Pour the batter into the hot pan. Bake for 10-12 minutes or until the cornbread is done in the center and golden brown.

Remove the cornbread from the oven and let the cornbread cool completely. When the cornbread is cool, cut the cornbread into 1/2" cubes. Place the cornbread cubes on a jelly roll pan in a single layer. Drizzle 1 tablespoon melted butter over the cornbread cubes. Toss until the cubes are coated in the butter.

Preheat the oven to 350°. Bake for 12-15 minutes or until the croutons are dried and lightly browned. Remove the croutons from the oven and serve warm.

Cheese Cornmeal Croutons

Makes 6 servings

2/3 cup cold water
2/3 cup plain white or yellow cornmeal
1/4 tsp. salt
2 cups boiling water
5 tbs. unsalted butter, softened
1/2 cup all purpose flour
1/2 cup shredded cheese (use your favorite flavor)

In a sauce pan over medium heat, add the cold water, cornmeal and salt. Stir until combined. Slowly stir in the boiling water. Continue stirring and cook until the cornmeal thickens and bubbles. Reduce the heat to low and simmer for 10 minutes. Stir frequently while the cornmeal cooks. Remove the pan from the heat.

Grease a 9 x 5 loaf pan with 1 tablespoon butter. Pour the cornmeal into the loaf pan. Place the pan in the refrigerator and chill about 6 hours. The cornmeal should be completely firm. When the cornmeal is ready, invert the pan to remove the cornmeal on your work surface. Cut the cornmeal into bite size croutons.

In a shallow bowl, add the all purpose flour. Roll each crouton in the flour. In a skillet over medium heat, add 2 tablespoons butter. When the butter melts, add part of the croutons. Do not crowd the skillet or the croutons will not brown. Cook for 3-5 minutes or until the croutons are browned. Turn the croutons frequently to brown all sides. Remove the croutons from the skillet and place in a bowl. Sprinkle part of the cheese over the hot croutons.

Repeat the cooking process until all the croutons are cooked. Add the remaining butter as needed to cook the remaining croutons. Serve with salads, soups, or stews.

Cornmeal Pastry

Use this pastry for a pot pie or savory meat pie. This makes enough crust for a 9 x 13 pan. You can roll the dough thinner for two 9" pie crust. We even use it for a pizza crust. You need to bake the crust for 5 minutes at 400° before using for a pizza crust.

1 cup all purpose flour
1/4 cup plain white or yellow cornmeal
1/2 tsp. salt
1/3 cup plus 1 tbs. vegetable shortening
3 tbs. cold water

In a mixing bowl, add the all purpose flour, cornmeal and salt. Stir until combined. Add the vegetable shortening to the bowl. Using a pastry blender, cut the shortening into the dry ingredients until the dough resembles coarse crumbs. You should still be able to see tiny pieces of the shortening when done.

Add the water and mix only until the dough comes together. I use my hands to mix the dough. You do not want to over work the dough or it will be tough. Lightly flour your work surface and roll the dough to your desired shape and thickness.

For pie crust, I roll to a little more than 1/8" thickness. Bake the crust at 400° until golden brown if desired.

Cornmeal Waffles

Makes about ten 4" waffles

1 1/2 cups self rising white or yellow cornmeal
1 1/2 cups self rising flour
1/4 cup granulated sugar
3 eggs, beaten
1 1/2 cups whole milk
1/4 cup melted unsalted butter

Preheat the waffle iron and grease with vegetable oil or non stick cooking spray. The waffle iron must be hot and greased or the waffles may stick. In a mixing bowl, add the cornmeal, self rising flour and granulated sugar. Whisk until combined. In a separate bowl, stir together the eggs, milk and butter. Add to the dry ingredients and mix only until the batter is moistened and combined.

Use about 1/4 to 1/2 cup batter for each waffle. The batter will vary based upon your waffle iron measurements. Do not over fill the waffle iron but place enough batter to make a full size waffle. Cook the waffle about 3 minutes or until done and golden brown. The waffle takes about 3 minutes on my waffle iron. It may take more or less time depending upon your waffle iron. Serve the waffle with a sweet or savory topping.

You can add up to 1 cup diced onions, bell peppers, jalapeño peppers, cooked meat or cheese to the waffle batter if desired. Use your imagination and make your favorite combination.

Cheddar Pecan Cornmeal Waffles

Makes about twelve 4" waffles

1 cup all purpose flour
1 cup plain white or yellow cornmeal
2 tsp. baking powder
1 tsp. baking soda
1/2 tsp. salt
1 1/2 cups shredded sharp cheddar cheese
1/2 cup chopped toasted pecans
3 eggs
1 cup buttermilk
1 cup club soda
1/3 cup vegetable oil

Preheat the waffle iron. In a mixing bowl, add the all purpose flour, cornmeal, baking powder, baking soda and salt. Stir until combined. Stir in the cheddar cheese and pecans.

In a separate bowl, whisk together the eggs, buttermilk, club soda and vegetable oil. Whisk until well combined and add to the dry ingredients. Mix only until the batter is combined.

Pour about 1/4 cup batter per waffle onto your hot waffle iron. Bake for 3-5 minutes or until the waffles are done and golden brown. Repeat until all the waffles are cooked.

Each waffle iron cooks differently and will hold a different amount of batter. Use the amount of batter called for in your waffle iron and adjust the cooking time as directed for your waffle iron. Most waffle irons use about 1/4 cup to 1/2 cup batter for waffles.

Corn Chile Waffles

Makes sixteen 4" waffles

3 eggs, separated and at room temperature
1 1/2 cups plain yellow cornmeal
1 1/2 cups all purpose flour
1 1/2 tsp. baking soda
1/4 tsp. salt
1/2 tsp. chili powder
1 cup cream style corn
2 1/4 cups buttermilk
4 oz. can diced green chiles, drained
1/3 cup melted unsalted butter

Preheat the waffle iron and grease with vegetable oil or non stick cooking spray. The waffle iron must be hot and greased or the waffles may stick.

In a mixing bowl, add the egg whites. Using a mixer on medium speed, beat the egg whites until stiff peaks form. In a separate mixing bowl, add the cornmeal, all purpose flour, baking soda, salt and chili powder. Whisk until combined. In a separate bowl, stir together the egg yolks, corn, buttermilk, green chiles and butter. Add to the dry ingredients and mix only until the batter is moistened and combined. Gently fold the beaten egg whites into the batter.

Use about 1/4 to 1/2 cup batter for each waffle. The batter will vary based upon your waffle iron measurements. Do not over fill the waffle iron but place enough batter to make a full size waffle. Cook the waffle about 3 minutes or until done and golden brown. The waffle takes about 3 minutes on my waffle iron. It may take more or less time depending upon your waffle iron. Serve the waffle with a sweet or savory topping.

Blue Cornmeal Blueberry Pancakes

Makes 24 pancakes

2 cups blue cornmeal
2 cups all purpose flour
1 1/2 tsp. baking soda
1/2 tsp. salt
3 eggs, beaten
2 1/2 cups buttermilk
1/3 cup honey
3 tbs. vegetable oil
1 1/2 cups fresh blueberries or frozen blueberries, thawed
2 tbs. granulated sugar

In a mixing bowl, add the blue cornmeal, all purpose flour, baking soda and salt. Stir until combined. In a separate bowl, add the eggs, buttermilk, honey and vegetable oil. Stir until well combined and add to the dry ingredients. Mix only until the batter is moistened. Let the batter rest for 10 minutes.

The cornmeal will absorb liquid while resting. Depending upon the brand cornmeal used, you may need to add additional liquid. Add milk as needed to make a thick but pourable batter.

When the batter has rested, gently fold in the blueberries and granulated sugar. Preheat a griddle or large skillet over medium heat. Spray the griddle with non stick cooking spray if desired. Use about 1/4 cup batter for each pancake. Cook the pancakes about 2 minutes on each side. The pancake edges should appear cooked and bubbles should be formed on the pancake when ready to flip.

Serve the pancakes with your favorite toppings.

Cornmeal Dumplings

Makes about 12 dumplings

1 egg, beaten
1/4 cup whole milk
1 tbs. vegetable oil
1/2 cup plain yellow cornmeal
1/4 tsp. poultry seasoning
1/2 cup all purpose flour
1 tsp. baking powder
1/2 tsp. salt

In a mixing bowl, add the egg, milk, vegetable oil and cornmeal. Mix until combined. Stir in the poultry seasoning, all purpose flour, baking powder and salt. Mix only until the batter is combined.

Drop the dumplings, by tablespoonfuls, onto any hot casserole, bubbling pot of beans, soup or stew. You can fry the dumplings in hot vegetable oil if desired.

Never drop dumpling batter onto a cold soup or casserole. The soup, stew or casserole should be hot when you add the dumplings. If you place dumplings on a cold stew, the dumplings will not cook properly.

Blue Corn Crepes

Makes 12 crepes

1/2 cup blue cornmeal
1/2 cup boiling water
1/2 cup all purpose flour
1/2 tsp. salt
3 eggs, beaten
3/4 cup whole milk
1 tbs. melted unsalted butter
Vegetable oil as needed

In a mixing bowl, add the cornmeal and boiling water. Stir until well combined. Allow the cornmeal to cool at room temperature. When the cornmeal is cool, stir in the all purpose flour, salt, eggs, milk and butter. Stir until smooth and combined.

Lightly grease a 6" skillet or crepe pan with vegetable oil. Place the skillet over medium heat. When the oil is hot, spoon 3 tablespoons batter into the pan. Tilt the skillet so the crepe covers the pan. Cook for 1 minute. Flip the crepe over and cook for 30-45 seconds or until the crepe is done.

Place the crepe on a clean dish towel to cool. Repeat until all the crepes are made. Place waxed paper between the crepes while making all the crepes. Stacking the crepes on top of each other will keep the crepes warm.

Fill with your favorite savory fillings. I like to fill them a thick beef stew or beans. You can substitute plain yellow cornmeal for the blue cornmeal if desired.

Mexican Cornbread Salad

Makes 8 servings

6 oz. pkg. Mexican cornbread mix
4 oz. can diced green chiles, drained
1/8 tsp. rubbed sage
1 oz. pkg. dry ranch salad dressing mix
1 cup sour cream
1 cup mayonnaise
4 cups cooked pinto beans
1 cup chopped green bell pepper
4 cups cooked whole kernel corn
3 large tomatoes, chopped
10 slices cooked bacon, crumbled
2 cups shredded cheddar cheese
1 cup sliced green onions

Prepare the cornbread mix according to the package directions but add the green chiles and sage to the batter. Bake as directed on the package. When the cornbread is done, crumble the cornbread into pieces.

In a small bowl, add the ranch salad dressing mix, sour cream and mayonnaise. Whisk until well combined. In a large shallow dish, crumble half of the cornbread into the bottom of the dish. Spoon half of the pinto beans, green bell pepper, corn, tomatoes, bacon, cheese and green onions over the cornbread.

Repeat the layering process one more time using the remaining cornbread, pinto beans, green bell pepper, corn, tomatoes, bacon, cheddar cheese and green onions. Spread the ranch dressing over the top. Cover the dish and refrigerate for 2 hours before serving.

Old Fashioned Hush Puppies

Makes about 2 dozen

1 cup plain white cornmeal
1/2 cup all purpose flour
2 tsp. baking powder
1 tsp. garlic salt
1/2 tsp. salt
1/2 cup minced onion
1 green onion, chopped
1 egg, beaten
1 cup whole milk
Vegetable oil for frying

In a mixing bowl, add the cornmeal, all purpose flour, baking powder, garlic salt, salt, onion, green onion, egg and milk. Whisk until well combined.

In a deep fryer or large sauce pan, add enough vegetable oil to at least a 2" depth. The oil needs to be heated to 370°. When the oil is hot, drop the batter, by tablespoonfuls, into the hot oil. Only cook a few hush puppies at a time. Do not over crowd the fryer or the temperature of the oil will drop and the hush puppies will not cook properly.

Fry the hush puppies about 2 minutes on each side or until done in the center and golden brown. Remove the hush puppies from the oil and drain on paper towels.

Keep cooked hush puppies warm in a 200° oven until all the hush puppies are done.

I cook a few hush puppies and then break them open to make certain the insides are done. I then cook the rest of the batch adjusting the time if needed to cook the remaining hush puppies.

Mexican Hush Puppies

Makes 2 dozen

3/4 cup plain yellow cornmeal
1/2 cup all purpose flour
1 1/2 tsp. baking powder
1/2 tsp. salt
1/8 tsp. cayenne pepper
1 cup shredded Monterey Jack cheese
4 oz. can diced green chiles, drained
1 tbs. minced onion
1 egg
1/2 cup whole milk
Vegetable oil for frying

In a mixing bowl, add the cornmeal, all purpose flour, baking powder, salt, cayenne pepper, Monterey Jack cheese, green chiles and onion. Stir until combined. Stir in the egg and milk. Mix only until combined and the batter is moistened.

In a deep fryer or large sauce pan, add enough vegetable oil to at least a 2" depth. The oil needs to be heated to 375°. When the oil is hot, drop the batter, by tablespoonfuls, into the hot oil. Only cook a few hush puppies at a time. Do not over crowd the fryer or the temperature of the oil will drop and the hush puppies will not cook properly.

Fry the hush puppies about 2 minutes on each side or until done and golden brown. Remove the hush puppies from the oil and drain on paper towels. Keep cooked hush puppies warm in a 200° oven until all the hush puppies are done.

I cook a few hush puppies and then break them open to make certain the insides are done. I then cook the rest of the batch adjusting the time if needed to cook the remaining hush puppies.

Bacon Hush Puppies

Makes about 18 hush puppies

6 slices bacon
1 1/2 cups plain yellow cornmeal
1/2 cup all purpose flour
1 tbs. baking powder
1/4 tsp. salt
1/2 cup chopped onion
1 egg, beaten
1 cup buttermilk
Vegetable oil for frying

In a skillet over medium heat, add the bacon. Cook about 6 minutes or until the bacon is crisp. Remove the bacon from the skillet and drain on paper towels. Crumble the bacon into pieces.

In a mixing bowl, add the cornmeal, all purpose flour, baking powder and salt. Stir until combined. Stir in the onion, bacon, egg and buttermilk. Mix only until the batter is moistened.

In a deep fryer or large sauce pan, add enough vegetable oil to at least a 2" depth. The oil needs to be heated to 370°. When the oil is hot, drop the batter, by tablespoonfuls, into the hot oil. Only cook a few hush puppies at a time. Do not over crowd the fryer or the temperature of the oil will drop and the hush puppies will not cook properly.

Fry the hush puppies about 2 minutes on each side or until done and golden brown. Remove the hush puppies from the oil and drain on paper towels. Keep cooked hush puppies warm in a 200° oven until all the hush puppies are done.

I cook a few hush puppies and then break them open to make certain the insides are done. I then cook the rest of the batch adjusting the time if needed to cook the remaining hush puppies.

Tomato Onion Hush Puppies

Makes about 2 dozen

7 oz. pkg. hush puppy mix (Martha White or Autrey's is our fave)
1 egg
2/3 cup buttermilk
1/2 cup chopped onion
1/2 cup chopped fresh tomato
Vegetable oil for frying

Add the hush puppy mix, egg, buttermilk, onion and tomato to a mixing bowl. Stir until well combined. Let the batter sit for 5 minutes. All hush puppy and cornbread batters will benefit from resting for a few minutes before cooking. Resting makes the batter lighter.

In a deep fryer or large sauce pan over medium high heat, add vegetable oil to a depth of 3". The temperature of the oil should be 375° when ready. When the oil is hot, drop the batter, by tablespoonfuls, into the hot oil. You will need to cook the hushpuppies in batches. If you add too many at one time to the hot oil, the temperature of the oil will drop and the hushpuppies will be greasy.

Fry the hush puppies about 2 minutes on each side or until the center of the hushpuppies are done and golden brown. Remove the hush puppies from the oil and drain on paper towels. Keep cooked hush puppies warm in a 200° oven until all the hush puppies are done.

I cook a few hush puppies and then break them open to make certain the insides are done. I then cook the rest of the batch adjusting the time if needed to cook the remaining hush puppies.

Fiery Beer Hush Puppies

Makes about 45 hush puppies

1 cup plain yellow cornmeal
1 cup all purpose flour
1 tsp. baking powder
1 tbs. granulated sugar
1 tsp. salt
2 eggs, beaten
1 cup beer
3/4 cup finely chopped onion
2 tbs. finely chopped jalapeño peppers
3 dashes Tabasco sauce
Vegetable oil for frying

In a mixing bowl, add the cornmeal, all purpose flour, baking powder, granulated sugar and salt. Whisk until combined. Stir in the eggs, beer, onion, jalapeño peppers and Tabasco sauce. Mix until the batter is combined.

In a deep fryer or deep skillet over medium high heat, add vegetable oil to a 2" depth in the pan. The temperature of the oil should be 365° when ready. Drop the batter, by teaspoonfuls, into the hot oil. You will need to fry the hushpuppies in batches. If you add too many at one time to the hot oil, the temperature of the oil will drop and the hushpuppies will be under cooked and greasy.

Fry about 1 minute on each side or until the hush puppies are done and golden brown. Remove the hush puppies from the oil and drain on paper towels. Keep cooked hush puppies warm in a 200° oven until all the hush puppies are done.

I cook a few hush puppies and then break them open to make certain the insides are done. I then cook the rest of the batch adjusting the time if needed to cook the remaining hush puppies.

Corn Hush Puppies

Makes about 25 hush puppies

1 cup all purpose flour
1 cup plain yellow or white cornmeal
2 tsp. baking powder
3/4 tsp. salt
3/4 cup cream style corn
1/2 cup chopped onion
1 egg, beaten
2 tbs. vegetable oil
Vegetable oil for frying

In a mixing bowl, add the all purpose flour, cornmeal, baking powder and salt. Whisk until well combined. Stir in the corn, onion, egg and 2 tablespoons vegetable oil. Whisk until well combined.

In a deep fryer or deep skillet over medium high heat, add enough vegetable oil to a depth of 2" in the pan. The temperature of the oil should be 370° when ready. Drop the batter, by tablespoonfuls, into the hot oil. You will need to cook the hushpuppies in batches. If you add too many at one time to the hot oil, the temperature of the oil will drop and the hushpuppies will be under cooked and greasy.

Fry about 2 minutes on each side or until the center is done and they are golden brown. Remove the hush puppies from the oil and drain on paper towels.

Keep cooked hush puppies warm in a 200° oven until all the hush puppies are done. I cook a few hush puppies and then break them open to make certain the insides are done. I then cook the rest of the batch adjusting the time if needed to cook the remaining hush puppies.

Mississippi Hush Puppies

Makes about 16 hush puppies

1 cup self rising white cornmeal
1/2 cup self rising flour
1 tbs. granulated sugar
1 egg, beaten
1/2 cup whole milk
1/2 cup diced onion
1/2 cup chopped green bell pepper
1 jalapeño pepper, seeded and chopped
Vegetable oil for frying

In a large mixing bowl, add the cornmeal, self rising flour and granulated sugar. Stir until combined. In a separate bowl, add the egg, milk, onion, green bell pepper and jalapeño pepper. Whisk until combined and add to the dry ingredients. Mix only until the batter is moistened and combined.

In a deep fryer or deep skillet over medium heat, add the vegetable oil to a depth of 2" in the pan. The temperature of the oil should be 375° when ready. Drop the batter, by tablespoonfuls, into the hot oil. You will need to cook the hushpuppies in batches. If you add too many at one time to the hot oil, the temperature of the oil will drop and the hushpuppies will be under cooked and greasy.

Fry about 2 minutes on each side or until the hush puppies are done and golden brown. Remove the hush puppies from the oil and drain on paper towels.

Keep cooked hush puppies warm in a 200° oven until all the hush puppies are done. I cook a few hush puppies and then break them open to make certain the insides are done. I then cook the rest of the batch adjusting the time if needed to cook the remaining hush puppies.

Squash Puppies

Makes 20 hush puppies

3/4 cup self rising cornmeal
1/4 cup all purpose flour
1/2 tsp. salt
1/4 tsp. black pepper
1/8 tsp. cayenne pepper
6 yellow squash, cooked and mashed
1/2 cup buttermilk
1/3 cup onion, minced
1 egg
Vegetable oil for frying

In a mixing bowl, add the cornmeal, all purpose flour, salt, black pepper and cayenne pepper. Stir until combined. In a separate bowl, stir together the squash, buttermilk, onion and egg. Whisk until well combined and add to the dry ingredients. Mix until combined.

In a deep skillet over medium high heat, add vegetable oil to a 1/2" depth in the skillet. The temperature of the oil should be 350° when ready. When the oil is hot, drop the batter by tablespoonfuls into the hot oil. Fry about 3 minutes on each side or until done and golden brown. Remove the hush puppies from the oil and drain on paper towels.

Sprinkle the hush puppies with additional salt and black pepper if desired.

Acorn Squash Puppies

Makes 2 dozen

1 3/4 lbs. acorn squash
2 cups self rising cornmeal
1/4 cup all purpose flour
1 egg, beaten
1/2 cup whole milk
1/2 cup finely chopped onion
Vegetable oil for frying

Preheat the oven to 375°. Cut the acorn squash in half crosswise. Remove the seeds from the squash. Place the squash halves, cut side down, in a shallow 9" baking pan. Add water to 1/2" in the pan. Bake the squash for 45 minutes or until the squash is tender. Remove the squash from the oven and let the squash cool completely before using.

Scoop out the squash from the shells. Discard the shells. Add the squash to a food processor. Process until smooth. Measure out 1 1/4 cups squash. You only need 1 1/4 cups squash to make the recipe. Save the remaining squash for another recipe.

In a mixing bowl, add the cornmeal and all purpose flour. Whisk until combined. In a separate bowl, add the squash, egg, milk and onion. Whisk until combined and add to the dry ingredients. Mix only until the batter is combined and moistened.

In a deep skillet over medium high heat, add vegetable oil to a 1/2" depth in the skillet. The temperature of the oil should be 350° when ready. When the oil is hot, drop the batter by tablespoonfuls into the hot oil. Fry about 2 minutes on each side or until golden brown. Remove the hush puppies from the oil and drain on paper towels.

Sprinkle the hush puppies with salt and black pepper if desired.

Shrimp Puppies

Makes 4 dozen

1/2 lb. shrimp, peeled, deveined and cooked
6 oz. pkg. Mexican cornbread mix
1/3 cup all purpose flour
8 oz. can cream style corn
1/4 cup chopped green onions
2 pickled jalapeño peppers, diced
1/4-1/2 cup whole milk as needed
Vegetable oil for frying

The shrimp need to be chilled before using in this recipe. Chop the shrimp before using. In a mixing bowl, add the cornbread mix and all purpose flour. Stir until combined. Add the shrimp, corn, green onions and jalapeño peppers. Mix only until the batter is combined. Depending upon the creaminess of the corn used, you may need to add the milk to make a thick but mixable batter. Only use the milk as needed.

In a deep skillet over medium high heat, add vegetable oil to a 2" depth in the skillet. The temperature of the oil should be 350° when ready. You will need to cook the hushpuppies in batches. If you add too many at one time, the temperature of the oil will drop and they will be under cooked and greasy. When the oil is hot, drop the batter by tablespoonfuls into the hot oil. Fry about 2 minutes on each side or until golden brown. Remove the hush puppies from the oil and drain on paper towels.

Keep cooked hush puppies warm in a 200° oven until all the hush puppies are done.

I cook a few hush puppies and then break them open to make certain the insides are done. I then cook the rest of the batch adjusting the time if needed to cook the remaining hush puppies.

Baked Hush Puppies

Makes 3 dozen

1 cup plain yellow cornmeal
1 cup all purpose flour
1 tbs. baking powder
1 tsp. granulated sugar
1 tsp. salt
1/8 tsp. cayenne pepper
2 eggs, beaten
3/4 cup whole milk
1/4 cup vegetable oil
1/2 cup finely chopped onion
Vegetable cooking spray

In a mixing bowl, add the cornmeal, all purpose flour, baking powder, granulated sugar, salt and cayenne pepper. Whisk until well blended. In a separate bowl, whisk together the eggs, milk, onion and vegetable oil. Add to the dry ingredients and whisk until combined.

Preheat the oven to 425°. Spray a miniature muffin pan with vegetable cooking spray. Spoon about 1 tablespoon batter into each muffin cup. Bake for 15 minutes or until the hush puppies are done and golden brown. Remove the pan from the oven and immediately remove from the pan. Serve hot.

Green Onion Tomato Hush Puppies

Makes about 3 dozen

1 cup plain yellow cornmeal
1/2 cup all purpose flour
1 1/2 tsp. baking powder
1 tsp. salt
1 tsp. granulated sugar
1/4 tsp. garlic powder
1/4 tsp. black pepper
1 egg, beaten
1/4 cup whole milk
1 tomato, chopped
3/4 cup diced green onions
Vegetable oil for frying

In a large mixing bowl, add the cornmeal, all purpose flour, baking powder, salt, granulated sugar, garlic powder and black pepper. Whisk until combined. Add the egg and milk. Mix only until combined. Gently fold in the tomato and green onions.

In a deep fryer or deep skillet over medium heat, add the vegetable oil to a depth of 2" in the pan. The temperature of the oil should be 360° when ready. Drop the batter, by tablespoonfuls, into the hot oil. You will need to cook the hushpuppies in batches. If you add too many at one time to the hot oil, the temperature of the oil will drop and the hushpuppies will be under cooked and greasy.

Fry about 2 minutes on each side or until the hush puppies are done and golden brown. Remove the hush puppies from the oil and drain on paper towels.

Keep cooked hush puppies warm in a 200° oven until all the hush puppies are done.

I cook a few hush puppies and then break them open to make certain the insides are done. I then cook the rest of the batch adjusting the time if needed to cook the remaining hush puppies.

Peppery Hush Puppies

Makes about 45 hush puppies

2 cups plain white or yellow cornmeal
1/2 cup pancake mix
1 tsp. baking powder
2 1/2 tsp. granulated sugar
1 tsp. salt
1/2 cup diced onion
1/2 cup diced green bell pepper
2 jalapeño peppers, seeded and diced
1 egg
1 cup buttermilk
2 tbs. vegetable oil
1/8 tsp. Tabasco sauce
Vegetable oil for frying

In a mixing bowl, add the cornmeal, pancake mix, baking powder, granulated sugar, salt, onion, green bell pepper and jalapeño peppers. Stir until combined. In a separate bowl, whisk together the egg, buttermilk, 2 tablespoons vegetable oil and Tabasco sauce. Add to the dry ingredients and mix only until combined.

In a deep fryer or deep skillet over medium heat, add the vegetable oil to a depth of 3" in the pan. The temperature of the oil should be 360° when ready. Drop the batter, by tablespoonfuls, into the hot oil. You will need to cook the hushpuppies in batches. If you add too many at one time to the hot oil, the temperature of the oil will drop and the hushpuppies will be under cooked and greasy.

Fry about 2 minutes on each side or until the hush puppies are done and golden brown. Remove the hush puppies from the oil and drain on paper towels.

Keep cooked hush puppies warm in a 200° oven until all the hush puppies are done.

I cook a few hush puppies and then break them open to make certain the insides are done. I then cook the rest of the batch adjusting the time if needed to cook the remaining hush puppies.

Aunt Jenny's Hush Puppies

Makes about 4 dozen

1 3/4 cups self rising white cornmeal
1 1/2 cups self rising flour
1 1/2 cups plain yellow cornmeal
2 tsp. baking powder
1/2 tsp. salt
1/2 tsp. garlic powder
3/4 tsp. cayenne pepper
1 1/2 cups whole milk
3/4 cup whole fat buttermilk
1 egg, beaten
1/2 cup minced onion
1/4 cup diced jalapeño peppers
Vegetable oil for frying

In a mixing bowl, add the white cornmeal, self rising flour, yellow cornmeal, baking powder, salt, garlic powder and cayenne pepper. Whisk until well blended. Stir in the whole milk, buttermilk, egg, onion and jalapeño peppers. Mix until well blended.

In a deep fryer or deep skillet over medium heat, add the vegetable oil to a depth of 3" in the pan. The temperature of the oil should be 370° when ready. Drop the batter, by tablespoonfuls, into the hot oil. You will need to cook the hushpuppies in batches. If you add too many at one time to the hot oil, the temperature of the oil will drop and the hushpuppies will be under cooked and greasy.

Fry about 2 minutes on each side or until the hush puppies are done and golden brown. Remove the hush puppies from the oil and drain on paper towels.

Keep cooked hush puppies warm in a 200° oven until all the hush puppies are done.

I cook a few hush puppies and then break them open to make certain the insides are done. I then cook the rest of the batch adjusting the time if needed to cook the remaining hush puppies.

Onion Cornbread Shortcake

This is so easy to make with package cornbread mix. You can substitute about 1 1/2 to 2 cups self rising cornmeal for the mix if desired.

1 large sweet onion, sliced
1/4 cup unsalted butter, melted
1 egg, beaten
1/3 cup whole milk
8 oz. can cream style corn
2 pkgs. cornbread muffin mix, 6 oz. size
1 tbs. vegetable shortening
1 cup sour cream
1/4 tsp. salt
1/4 tsp. dried dill
1 cup shredded sharp cheddar cheese

In a skillet over medium heat, add the onion and butter. Saute the onion about 5 minutes or until tender. Remove the skillet from the heat. In a mixing bowl, add the egg, milk and cream style corn. Whisk until well blended. Stir in the cornbread muffin mix. Stir only until the batter is moistened. Preheat the oven to 350°. Place the vegetable shortening in an 8" square pan. Place the pan in the oven until the shortening is melted and sizzling hot. Pour the batter into the prepared pan.

In a mixing bowl, add the sour cream, salt, dill and 1/2 cup cheddar cheese. Stir until well combined and spread over the batter. Bake for 25 minutes. Sprinkle the remaining 1/2 cup cheese over the top of the cornbread. Bake for 5-10 minutes or until the cornbread is done in the center and the cheese melted and bubbly. Remove the pan from the oven and cut into squares. Serve with any meat or soup.

Green Onion Hoecakes

Makes 8 servings

1 egg, beaten
1 1/2 cups self rising cornmeal
1 1/4 cups buttermilk
1/4 cup chopped green onions
1/2 cup plus 1 tbs. vegetable oil

In a mixing bowl, add the egg, cornmeal, buttermilk, green onions and 1 tablespoon vegetable oil. Whisk until well combined. In a large skillet over medium heat, add 1/2 cup vegetable oil. When the vegetable oil is hot, add 1/4 cup batter for each cake to the skillet. Cook about 3-4 minutes on each side or until done and golden brown.

You will need to cook the hoecakes in two batches. If you do not have a large skillet, cook in additional batches. The hoecakes should be well browned and bubbles formed on the top before flipping the cake. Remove the hoecakes from the skillet and drain on paper towels. Sprinkle salt and black pepper over the hoecakes if desired. Add additional vegetable oil if needed to fry all the hoecakes.

Lacy Corn Cakes

Makes about 2 dozen

2 eggs. well beaten
2 cups whole milk
1/4 cup plus 3 tbs. vegetable oil
1 1/3 cups plain yellow cornmeal
3/4 tsp. salt

In a mixing bowl, add the eggs, milk and 1/4 cup vegetable oil. Whisk until well combined. Stir in the cornmeal and salt. Mix only until combined. You will have to fry the corn cakes in batches. Stir the cornbread batter each time before adding to the skillet.

Add 1 tablespoon vegetable oil to a skillet over medium heat. When the oil is hot, drop 2 tablespoons batter for each cake into the hot skillet. The edges will take on a lacy appearance and look cooked when they are ready to flip. The top of the cake should also be bubbly. Cook about 2 minutes per side or until golden brown.

Remove the cakes from the skillet and add another tablespoon vegetable oil as needed to cook the rest of the corn cakes. Serve the corn cakes hot.

Southern Corn Cakes

Makes about 8 corn cakes

1 1/2 cups self rising cornmeal
1 tbs. granulated sugar
1 cup buttermilk
1 egg, beaten
5 tbs. vegetable oil

In a mixing bowl, add the cornmeal, granulated sugar, buttermilk, egg and 1 tablespoon vegetable oil. Whisk until well combined.

Add 3 tablespoons vegetable oil to a large skillet over medium heat. When the oil is hot and shimmering, add 1/4 cup batter for each pancake. Fry the corn cakes about 3 minutes on each side. The corn cakes should be golden brown on the bottom and bubbly on top when they are ready to flip. Add the additional tablespoon vegetable oil if needed to fry all the corn cakes. Remove the cakes from the skillet and serve hot.

Hearty Cornmeal Pancakes

Makes 20 pancakes

2 cups self rising flour
1/2 cup plain yellow or white cornmeal
2 tsp. baking soda
2 eggs, beaten
3 cups buttermilk
1/4 cup vegetable oil

In a mixing bowl, add the self rising flour, cornmeal and baking soda. Whisk until well combined. In a separate bowl, stir together the eggs, buttermilk and vegetable oil. Add to the dry ingredients and mix only until combined.

Preheat a griddle or skillet over medium heat. Spray the griddle with non stick cooking spray. Use 1/4 cup batter for each pancake. Pour the batter onto the hot griddle. Cook about 2-3 minutes per side. When the bottom of the pancakes are golden brown and the top bubbly, the pancakes are ready to flip.

Remove the pancakes from the griddle and serve with butter, yogurt, syrup or pureed fruit if desired.

Spinach Cornbread Bake

Makes 8 servings

1 1/2 cups self rising cornmeal
2 eggs
1 cup sour cream
10 oz. can condensed French onion soup
10 oz. pkg. frozen spinach, thawed and patted dry
1/2 cup melted unsalted butter
1/2 cup shredded sharp cheddar cheese

Preheat the oven to 350°. Spray a 12 x 8 x 2 baking dish with non stick cooking spray. In a mixing bowl, add the cornmeal, eggs, sour cream, French onion soup, spinach and melted butter. Whisk until well combined.

Spoon the batter into the prepared pan. Bake for 25 minutes. The casserole should be done in the center but still moist. Sprinkle the cheese over the top and bake for 5 minutes. The cheese should be melted and bubbly when done. Remove the dish from the oven and serve.

Garlic Spoon Bread

Makes 6 servings

1/4 cup plus 1 tbs. unsalted butter, softened
3/4 cup plain yellow or white cornmeal
1 1/2 cups water
2 cups shredded cheddar cheese
2 garlic cloves, crushed
1/2 tsp. salt
1 cup whole milk
5 egg yolks, beaten
1/2 lb. bacon, cooked and crumbled
4 egg whites, beaten to stiff peaks
3 tbs. finely chopped green onions, optional

Preheat the oven to 325°. Grease a 3 quart casserole dish with 1 tablespoon butter. In a large sauce pan over medium heat, add the cornmeal and water. Stir constantly and cook until the cornmeal thickens. This takes about 8 minutes on my stove. Remove the pan from the heat.

Stir in the cheddar cheese, 1/4 cup butter, garlic and salt. Stir until the cheese melts. In a small bowl, whisk together the milk and egg yolks. Stir into the cornmeal. Add the bacon and stir until combined. Gently fold in the beaten egg whites. Spoon the batter into the prepared casserole dish. Bake for 50-55 minutes or until the center of the spoon bread is set and tender. Remove the dish from the oven and sprinkle green onions over the top if desired.

Mushroom Spoon Bread

Makes 4 servings

1 1/2 cups whole milk
10.75 oz. can cream of mushroom soup
1 cup plain yellow cornmeal
2 tbs. unsalted butter
4 eggs, separated and at room temperature

In a large sauce pan over medium heat, add the milk and cream of mushroom soup. Stir until well combined. Stir constantly and add the cornmeal. Continue stirring and cook until the cornmeal thickens and begins to boil. Remove the pan from the heat. Add the butter and stir until the butter melts.

In a small bowl, add the egg yolks. Whisk until well combined. Add 1/4 cup cornmeal batter to the egg yolks. Whisk until combined and add to the sauce pan. Whisk until well smooth and combined.

In a mixing bowl, add the egg whites. Using a mixer on high speed, beat the egg whites until stiff peaks form. Fold the egg whites into the batter. Preheat the oven to 350°. Spray a 2 quart casserole dish with non stick cooking spray. Spoon the batter into the baking dish. Bake for 50-60 minutes. The spoon bread will be ready when the center of the bread springs back lightly when touched. Remove the dish from the oven and serve immediately.

Corn and Bacon Spoon Bread

Makes 12 servings

3/4 cup plain yellow cornmeal
1 1/2 cups water
2 cups shredded cheddar cheese
1 1/2 cups cooked whole kernel corn
1/4 cup unsalted butter
2 garlic cloves, minced
1 cup whole milk
1 tsp. salt
10 bacon slices, cooked and crumbled
4 eggs, separated and at room temperature

In a large sauce pan over medium heat, add the cornmeal and water. Stir constantly and bring the cornmeal to a boil. Cook for 1 minute or until the cornmeal thickens. Remove the pan from the heat and stir in the cheddar cheese, corn, butter, garlic, milk and salt. Whisk until well combined and the cheese and butter are melted. Stir in the crumbled bacon.

In a mixing bowl, add the egg yolks. Using a mixer on medium speed, beat the egg yolks for 3 minutes or until lemon colored. Add the egg yolks to the batter and stir until combined. In a separate bowl, add the egg whites. Using a mixer on medium speed, beat the egg whites until stiff peaks form. Gently fold the egg whites into the batter.

Preheat the oven to 325°. Spray a 2 1/2 quart casserole dish with non stick cooking spray. Spoon the batter into the prepared baking dish. Bake for 1 hour or until a knife inserted in the center of the spoon bread comes out clean. Remove the dish from the oven and serve.

Old Fashioned Southern Spoon Bread

Makes 6 servings

1 cup yellow or white plain cornmeal
1 1/2 tsp. salt
1 cup water
2 cups hot whole milk
2 eggs, beaten
3 tbs. melted vegetable shortening

In a sauce pan over low heat, add the cornmeal, salt, water and milk. Stir constantly and cook until the cornmeal is thickened and smooth. This takes about 10 minutes on my stove.

In a small bowl, add the beaten eggs. Add 2 tablespoons hot cornmeal batter to the eggs and whisk until combined. Add the eggs and melted vegetable shortening to the cornmeal batter in the pan. Stir until combined and remove the pan from the heat.

Preheat the oven to 375°. Spray a 1 1/2 quart casserole dish with non stick cooking spray. Spoon the cornmeal batter into the casserole dish. Bake for 40-45 minutes or until spoon bread should is set in the center and creamy. Remove the dish from the oven and serve.

Cheese Spoon Bread

Makes 8 servings

2 cups whole milk
1 cup plain yellow or white cornmeal
1/4 cup unsalted butter, melted
1/2 cup shredded cheddar cheese
4 eggs, separated and at room temperature
1 tsp. salt

In the top of a double boiler over medium heat, add the milk. Cook until the milk is hot but not boiling. Stir in the cornmeal. Stir constantly and cook until the cornmeal thickens. Remove the pan from the heat and stir in the butter, cheddar cheese, egg yolks and salt. Stir until the cheese melts and all the ingredients are well combined. Remove the pan from the heat.

In a mixing bowl, add the egg whites. Using a mixer on medium speed, beat until stiff peaks form. Depending upon your mixer, this may take anywhere from 3-8 minutes. Gently fold the beaten egg whites into the cornmeal batter.

Preheat the oven to 350°. Spray a 2 quart casserole dish with non stick cooking spray. Spoon the cornmeal batter into the dish. Bake for 30-35 minutes or until the spoon bread is puffed and golden brown. Remove the dish from the oven and serve immediately as the spoon bread will deflate when removed from the oven.

Cornbread Vegetable Supper

Makes 4 servings

1 cup plain yellow cornmeal
2 tsp. baking soda
1 tsp. salt
14 oz. can cream style corn
2 eggs, beaten
3/4 cup whole milk
1/4 cup vegetable oil
1 lb. ground beef
1 onion, chopped
15 oz. can cut green beans, drained
14 oz. can diced tomatoes with garlic and onion, drained
1/2 tsp. lemon pepper
2 cups shredded cheddar cheese

In a mixing bowl, add the cornmeal, baking soda, salt, corn, eggs, milk and vegetable oil. Stir until the batter is moistened and combined. Preheat the oven to 425°. Spray a shallow 2 1/2 quart casserole dish with non stick cooking spray. Pour the batter into the prepared baking dish.

In a skillet over medium heat, add the ground beef and onion. Stir the ground beef frequently to break the meat into crumbles as it cooks. Cook about 7 minutes or until the ground beef is browned and no longer pink. Drain off the excess grease.

Stir in the green beans, tomatoes and lemon pepper. Stir constantly and cook until the dish is hot and bubbly. Remove the skillet from the heat and pour over the batter in the baking dish. Sprinkle the cheddar cheese over the top. Bake for 15-20 minutes or until the cornbread is done and the casserole hot and bubbly. Remove the dish from the oven and serve.

Cornbread Stuffed Peppers

Makes 4 servings

6 oz. pkg. Mexican cornbread mix, prepared, cooked and cooled
1/2 cup diced onion
1/2 cup diced celery
1 yellow bell pepper, diced
1/2 cup diced cooked ham
1 tbs. olive oil
1/2 cup whole milk
1/2 cup buttermilk
1 tbs. chopped fresh thyme
2 eggs, beaten
1 1/2 cups chopped toasted pecans
1/4 tsp. salt
1/4 tsp. black pepper
8 red bell peppers
1/3 cup unsalted butter, cut into 16 pieces

Crumble the cornbread into a mixing bowl. In a skillet over medium heat, add the onion, celery, yellow bell pepper, ham and olive oil. Stir constantly and saute the vegetables and ham for 5 minutes or until the vegetables are tender. Reduce the heat to low.

Stir in the cornbread, milk, buttermilk and thyme. Remove the skillet from the heat. Stir in the eggs, pecans, salt and black pepper. Mix until well combined. Cut the red bell peppers in half crosswise. Remove the stem, seeds and membrane. Place the peppers in a 9 x 13 baking dish.

Preheat the oven to 375°. Spoon the cornbread filling into each red bell pepper half. Place the butter pieces over the top of each pepper. Bake for 20 minutes or until the filling is hot, set and lightly browned. Remove the peppers from the oven and serve.

Tamale Meatballs

My family loves these meatballs. They are slightly spicy but so good!

Makes about 6 dozen small meatballs

1 1/2 lbs. ground beef
2 cups crumbled cooked cornbread
10 oz. can mild enchilada sauce
1/2 tsp. salt
1 cup tomato sauce
1/2 cup shredded Monterey Jack Cheese

You can use cold leftover cornbread for this recipe. Preheat the oven to 350°. In a mixing bowl, add the ground beef, cornbread, 1/2 cup enchilada sauce and salt. Using your hands, mix until well combined. Use about a teaspoon meat and form into 1" meatballs. Place the meatballs on a large baking pan. Bake for 18-20 minutes or until the meatballs are browned and no longer pink.

Remove the pan from the oven and drain the meatballs on paper towels. Place the meatballs in a warming dish to keep warm while you prepare the sauce. In a sauce pan over low heat, add the remaining enchilada sauce and tomato sauce. Stir constantly and cook only until the sauce is heated. Pour the sauce over the meatballs. Sprinkle the cheese over the hot sauce and serve.

Cornbread Tamale Pie

Makes 6 servings

1 lb. ground beef
1 cup chopped onion
1 cup chopped green bell pepper
1 garlic clove, minced
2 cups tomato sauce
1 1/2 cups cooked whole kernel corn
15 black olives, sliced
1 tbs. granulated sugar
1 tbs. chili powder
1/8 tsp. salt
1/4 tsp. black pepper
1 cup shredded cheddar cheese
3/4 cup plain yellow cornmeal
2 cups water
1/2 tsp. salt
1 tbs. unsalted butter

In a skillet over medium heat, add the ground beef, onion, green bell pepper and garlic. Stir frequently to break the meat into crumbles as it cooks. Cook about 6 minutes or until the ground beef is browned and no longer pink. Drain all the excess grease from the skillet. Add the tomato sauce, corn, black olives, granulated sugar, chili powder, salt and black pepper to the skillet. Stir until well combined. Reduce the heat to low and simmer for 15 minutes. Remove the skillet from the heat and stir in the cheddar cheese.

Spray an 8" square baking pan with non stick cooking spray. Spoon the meat filling into the baking pan. Preheat the oven to 375°. In a sauce pan over medium heat, add the cornmeal, water and salt. Stir constantly and cook until the cornmeal thickens and bubbles. This takes about 3 minutes after the water boils on my stove. Remove the pan from the heat and stir in the butter. Spoon the cornmeal batter over the top of the ground beef.

Bake for 40 minutes or until the cornbread is golden brown and the casserole bubbly. Remove the dish from the oven and let the pie rest for 5 minutes before serving.

Easy Creamed Chicken over Cornbread

Makes 6 servings

1 1/2 tbs. vegetable shortening or bacon drippings
1 cup plain yellow cornmeal
3/4 cup plus 2 tbs. all purpose flour
2 tsp. baking powder
1 tsp. salt
2 1/2 cups whole milk
1 egg, beaten
1/4 cup vegetable oil
2 tbs. unsalted butter
3 cups cooked chicken, cubed
10.75 oz. can cream of mushroom soup
2 oz. jar diced red pimento, drained
1 cup shredded cheddar cheese
1/2 cup green onions

Preheat the oven to 425°. Add the vegetable shortening to an 8" square pan. Place the pan in the oven until the shortening melts and begins to sizzle. While the shortening is melting, make the cornbread. In a mixing bowl, add the cornmeal, 3/4 cup all purpose flour, baking powder and salt. Stir until combined. Whisk in 1 cup milk, egg and the vegetable oil. Mix until well combined.

Remove the hot pan from the oven. Pour the cornbread batter in the hot pan. Bake for 20 minutes or until the cornbread is done and lightly browned. While the cornbread is baking, make the chicken. In a sauce pan over medium heat, add the butter. When the butter melts, stir in 2 tablespoons all purpose flour. Stir constantly and cook for 1 minute. Slowly add 1 1/2 cups milk to the pan. Continue stirring and cook until the gravy thickens and bubbles. Stir in the chicken, cream of mushroom soup and red pimento. Cook only until thoroughly heated. Remove the pan from the heat.

When ready to serve, place a square of cornbread on each plate. Slice the cornbread in half horizontally. Spoon the chicken filling over each piece of cornbread. Sprinkle the cheddar cheese and green onions over each serving.

Sausage Cornbread Dressing

Makes a 9 x 13 baking dish

1 lb. ground pork sausage
2 onions, diced
4 stalks celery, diced
5 cups crumbled cooked cornbread
3 cups toasted white bread cubes
2 tsp. rubbed sage
1/2 tsp. black pepper
3 to 3 1/2 cups chicken broth
2 eggs, beaten

Preheat the oven to 350°. Spray a 9 x 13 baking dish with non stick cooking spray. In a skillet over medium heat, add the pork sausage, onions and celery. Stir frequently to break the sausage into crumbles as it cooks. Cook about 7-8 minutes or until the sausage is done and no longer pink. Drain off the excess grease.

In a large mixing bowl, add the sausage filling, cornbread, bread cubes, rubbed sage, black pepper, 3 cups chicken broth and 2 eggs. Use your hands or a heavy spoon and mix until combined. Add the remaining 1/2 cup chicken broth if needed to make a moist dressing.

The cornbread and bread will absorb additional liquid when baked. You need the dressing to be moist but not soupy. Spoon the dressing into the prepared baking dish. Bake for 30 minutes or until the dressing is hot and just begins to brown on the top. Remove the dressing from the oven and let the dressing rest for 5 minutes before serving.

Sage Cornbread Dressing

Makes 8 servings

3 cups crumbled cooked cornbread
2 cups crumbled stale bread
2 cups chicken broth
2 hard boiled eggs, chopped
2 onions, finely chopped
1 cup celery, finely chopped
1/2 cup unsalted butter, melted
1 tbs. dried whole sage, crumbled

Preheat the oven to 325°. Spray a 9 x 13 baking dish with non stick cooking spray. Add all the ingredients to the baking dish. Stir until well combined. Spread the dressing evenly over the pan. Bake for 1 hour or until the dressing is golden brown on top.

Green Chile Cornbread Dressing

Makes 8 servings

1/4 cup unsalted butter
2 cups chopped onions
1 cup chopped celery
1 3/4 cups chicken broth
16 oz. can whole kernel corn, drained
8 oz. can diced green chiles, drained
3 tbs. chopped fresh parsley
1/2 tsp. salt
1/2 tsp. poultry seasoning
1/4 tsp. dried oregano
1/4 tsp. black pepper
6 cups crumbled cornbread
1/2 cup toasted chopped pecans

In a large dutch oven over medium heat, add the butter, onions and celery. Saute for 5 minutes or until the vegetables are tender. Stir in the chicken broth, corn, green chiles, parsley, salt, poultry seasoning, oregano and black pepper. Bring to a boil and remove the pan from the heat.

Preheat the oven to 350°. Spray a 9 x 13 baking pan with non stick cooking spray. Add the cornbread and pecans to the baking pan. Pour the hot chicken broth over the cornbread. Toss until combined. Cover the dish with aluminum foil. Bake for 30 minutes or until the dressing is hot. Remove the pan from the oven and serve.

Granny's Cornbread Dressing

Makes 8 servings

2 cups self rising flour
1 cup self rising white cornmeal
2 cups buttermilk
3 eggs
1/2 cup unsalted butter, melted
1 cup chopped celery
2 medium onions, chopped
1 jalapeño pepper, seeded and chopped
1/4 tsp. black pepper
2 to 3 cups chicken broth
1/4 tsp. paprika, optional

In a large bowl, add the self rising flour and cornmeal. Whisk until combined. In a separate bowl, whisk together the buttermilk, eggs and butter. Add to the dry ingredients and stir until combined.

Preheat the oven to 400°. Spray a 9" square baking pan with non stick cooking spray. Pour the cornbread batter into the pan. Bake for 25 minutes or until the cornbread is done in the center and lightly browned. The cornbread will be lighter in color than cornbread used in other recipes. Remove the pan from the oven and cool completely before using.

Crumble the cornbread in a large mixing bowl. Add the celery, onions, jalapeño pepper, black pepper and 2 cups chicken broth. Stir until well combined. You need a moist dressing but not a soupy dressing. Add the remaining chicken broth if needed to make a moist dressing.

Preheat the oven to 350°. Spray a 11 x 7 baking dish with non stick cooking spray. Spoon the dressing into the pan. Bake for 20-25 minutes or until the dressing is lightly browned. Sprinkle the paprika over the top if desired. This dressing will not be golden brown. The dressing will be set, hot and lightly browned on top when ready.

Squash Cornbread Dressing

Makes 4 servings

2 cups sliced yellow squash
1 onion, chopped
1 cup water
2 cups cooked cornbread, crumbled
10.75 oz. can cream of chicken soup
1/4 cup melted unsalted butter
1/2 tsp. black pepper

In a sauce pan over medium heat, add the squash, onion and water. Bring the squash to a boil and reduce the heat to low. Place a lid on the pan and simmer about 10 minutes or until the squash is tender. Remove the pan from the heat and drain off any liquid. Using a potato masher, mash the squash and onions. Stir in the crumbled cornbread, cream of chicken soup, butter and black pepper.

Preheat the oven to 350°. Spray a 1 1/2 quart casserole dish with non stick cooking spray. Spoon the dressing into the casserole dish. Bake for 25-30 minutes or until the dressing is hot and set. Remove the dish from the oven and serve.

Note: You can substitute one 6 oz. pkg. Mexican cornbread mix baked for the cornbread if desired.

Kentucky Cornbread Dressing

Makes 8 servings

3 cups cooked cornbread, crumbled
2 cups soft white breadcrumbs
1 1/2 cups whole milk
1/3 cup melted bacon drippings
1 egg
1 cup chopped onion
3/4 cup raisins
1 tsp. rubbed sage
1/2 tsp. salt

Preheat the oven to 350°. Spray an 8" square pan with non stick cooking spray. Add all the ingredients to a large mixing bowl. Stir until well combined. Depending upon the dryness of your bread, you may need additional milk. Add a tablespoon or two additional milk if needed to make a moist dressing. You want the dressing moist but not soupy.

Spoon the dressing into the baking dish. Bake for 30-40 minutes or until the dressing is hot and lightly browned. Remove the dish from the oven and serve.

Old Fashioned Cornbread Dressing

Makes a 9 x 13 baking dish

1/2 cup plus 2 tbs. vegetable oil
2 cups plain yellow or white cornmeal
1 tbs. granulated sugar
1 tbs. baking powder
1 tsp. salt
5 eggs, beaten
12 oz. can evaporated milk
2 cups chopped fresh mushrooms
1 cup chopped celery
1/2 cup chopped green onion
3 tbs. unsalted butter, melted
3 1/2 cups chicken broth
10.75 oz. can cream of chicken soup
3/4 cup chopped pecans
1 tsp. poultry seasoning
1/2 tbs. black pepper
1/8 tsp. dried parsley flakes

Preheat the oven to 350°. Grease a 10" cast iron skillet with 2 tablespoons vegetable oil. Place the skillet in the oven for 4 minutes. The skillet should be sizzling hot and the oil should begin to sizzle when ready. In a large mixing bowl, add the cornmeal, granulated sugar, baking powder and salt. Stir until well combined. Stir in 2 eggs, evaporated milk and 1/2 cup vegetable oil. Whisk until well combined.

Spoon the batter into the hot skillet. Bake about 35-40 minutes or until the cornbread is done in the center and golden brown. Remove the cornbread from the oven and cool completely. When the cornbread is cool, crumble the cornbread into a large bowl.

In a skillet over medium heat, add the mushrooms, celery, green onion and melted butter. Stir frequently and saute the vegetables for 5 minutes. Remove the pan from the heat and pour the vegetables over the cornbread in the bowl. Add 3 beaten eggs, chicken broth, cream of chicken soup, pecans, poultry seasoning, black pepper and parsley flakes to the bowl. Stir until well combined.

Preheat the oven to 350°. Spray a 9 x 13 baking dish with non stick cooking spray. Spoon the dressing into the dish. Bake for 45 minutes or until the dressing is hot and lightly browned. Remove the pan from the oven and serve.

Oyster Cornbread Dressing

Makes a 11 x 7 baking dish

2 tbs. bacon drippings
1 cup all purpose flour
1 cup plain yellow cornmeal
1 tbs. baking powder
2 tsp. salt
2 1/2 cups whole milk
4 eggs
1/2 cup unsalted butter
1/2 cup chopped onion
3/4 cup chopped green bell pepper
1/2 cup chopped celery
3 bay leaves
2 tsp. minced garlic
12 oz. fresh oysters, undrained
1 cup chicken broth
1 tsp. black pepper
1/4 cup chopped green onions
2 tbs. finely chopped parsley
2 tsp. Tabasco sauce
1/2 tsp. dried thyme

You have to make the cornbread before you can make the dressing. To make the cornbread, preheat the oven to 375°. Add the bacon drippings to a 10" cast iron skillet. Place the skillet in the oven to heat for 5 minutes or until the drippings melt and the skillet is sizzling hot.

While the skillet is heating, make the batter. In a mixing bowl, add the all purpose flour, cornmeal, baking powder and 1 teaspoon salt. Stir until combined. Add 1 cup milk and 1 egg. Whisk until well combined. Pour the batter into the hot skillet. Bake for 20 minutes or until the cornbread is done in the center and golden brown. Remove the cornbread from the oven and cool completely before using.

In a skillet over medium heat, add the butter. When the butter melts, add the onion, green bell pepper, celery, bay leaves and garlic. Saute the vegetables for 4 minutes or until tender. Drain the oysters but reserve the liquid. Add the oyster liquid, chicken broth, black pepper and green onions to the skillet. Simmer for 5 minutes. Stir in the oysters, parsley, Tabasco sauce, 1 teaspoon salt and thyme. Remove the bay leaves and discard. Remove the skillet from the heat.

In a large mixing bowl, whisk together 3 eggs and 1 1/2 cups milk. Crumble the cornbread into the milk and eggs. Add the oyster mixture and toss until combined. Preheat the oven to 350°. Spray a 11 x 7 baking dish with non stick cooking spray. Spoon the dressing into the baking dish. Bake for 45 minutes or until the dressing is set and lightly browned. Remove the dressing from the oven and serve.

2 GRITS

Polenta with Sausage

Makes 4 servings

2 quarts water
1 tbs. salt
2 cups plain yellow cornmeal
1 lb. sweet Italian sausage, sliced
15 oz. can tomato paste
3 1/2 cups beef broth
1/2 tsp. rubbed sage
1/2 cup freshly grated Parmesan cheese

In a 4 quart sauce pan over medium heat, add the water and salt. Bring the water to a boil. When the water is boiling, whisk in cornmeal. Stir frequently and cook about 20-30 minutes or until the polenta is the consistency of mashed potatoes. Remove the polenta from the heat and keep warm while you prepare the rest of the recipe.

In a large skillet over medium heat, add the Italian sausage. Saute the sausage for 5 minutes. Drain off any excess grease. Stir in the tomato paste, beef broth and sage. Stir frequently and reduce the heat to low. Simmer about 30 minutes or until the sauce is thick. Spoon the polenta onto a serving platter. Spoon the sausage sauce over the polenta. Sprinkle the Parmesan cheese over the top and serve.

Grilled Polenta with Black Bean Salsa

Makes 4 servings

4 cups chicken broth
1 cup plain yellow cornmeal
2 cups cooked black beans, drained and rinsed
3/4 cup finely chopped tomato
1/2 cup finely chopped onion
1/2 cup finely chopped red bell pepper
1/4 cup chopped fresh cilantro
1 tsp. finely chopped jalapeño pepper
1/3 cup red wine vinegar

In a sauce pan over medium heat, add the chicken broth. Bring the chicken broth to a boil. When the broth is boiling, slowly whisk in the cornmeal. Stir frequently and reduce the heat to low. Simmer about 20 minutes or until the polenta is tender and thick.

Spray a 9" baking pan with non stick cooking spray. Spread the polenta into the baking pan. Refrigerate the polenta until firm. To grill the polenta, you will need to use a grill basket or grill pan. Spray the pan with non stick cooking spray. Cut the polenta into 4 squares. Place the polenta on the pan. Grill over hot coals about 5 minutes on each side or until the polenta is golden brown.

You can use an indoor grill pan to cook the polenta if desired. To make the black bean salsa, add the black beans, tomato, onion, red bell pepper, cilantro, jalapeño pepper and red wine vinegar to a mixing bowl. Toss until well combined. Chill the salsa if desired. Serve the black bean salsa over the polenta squares.

Baked Okra & Cheese Polenta

Makes a 11 x 7 baking dish

4 cups water
6 small fresh okra pods
1 cup quick cooking grits
1/2 tsp. salt
2 eggs, beaten
1/4 cup unsalted butter, cut into small pieces
8 oz. sharp cheddar cheese, cubed

In a large sauce pan over medium heat, add 2 cups water. Bring the water to a boil and add the okra. Cook the okra about 10 minutes or until tender. Remove the okra from the pan using a slotted spoon. Leave the water in the pan.

Cool the okra for 5 minutes. Cut the okra into slices. Add 2 cups water to the liquid in the sauce pan. Bring the water to a boil and stir in the grits and salt. Stir constantly and bring the grits to a boil. Reduce the heat to low and place a lid on the pan. Simmer the grits about 6 minutes or until tender.

In a small bowl, add the beaten eggs. Stir about 1/4 cup of the grits into the eggs. Whisk until well combined. Stir constantly and add the eggs to the pan. Whisk quickly so the eggs do not scramble. Stir in the butter and whisk until the butter melts. Remove the pan from the heat.

Preheat the oven to 350°. Spray a 11x 7 baking dish with non stick cooking spray. Stir the cheddar cheese and okra into the grits. Stir until the cheese is mostly melted. Pour the grits into the baking dish. Bake for 50-60 minutes or until the casserole is set in the center. Remove the dish from the oven and cool for 5 minutes before serving.

Skillet Polenta Squares

Makes 8 servings

2 cups water
2 cups chicken broth
1/2 cup whipping cream
2 cups plain white cornmeal
1 cup shredded Monterey Jack cheese
Vegetable oil for frying

In a large sauce pan over medium heat, add the water and chicken broth. Bring the liquids to a boil. When the liquids are boiling, slowly stir in 1 cup cornmeal. Whisk constantly and bring the cornmeal back to a boil. When the cornmeal boils, reduce the heat to low. Stir constantly and cook for 5 minutes. Stir in the whipping cream and simmer the polenta for 20 minutes. Stir occasionally while the polenta cooks to keep the cornmeal from sticking to the bottom of the pan. Remove the pan from the heat and stir in the Monterey Jack cheese.

Spray a 9" square pan with non stick cooking spray. Pour the polenta into the pan. Cover the pan and chill until firm. When the polenta is firm, turn the polenta out onto your work surface. Cut the polenta into 8 squares.

Place 1 cup cornmeal in a shallow dish. Dredge the polenta squares in the cornmeal. In a skillet over medium heat, add vegetable oil to a depth of 1/2" in the skillet. When the oil is hot, add the polenta squares. Fry for 2-3 minutes on each side or until golden brown. Remove the skillet from the heat. Remove the polenta and drain on paper towels. Top the polenta with your favorite toppings such as salsa, sour cream, butter, syrup or jelly.

Sage Pan Fried Polenta

Makes 8 servings

1/2 cup unsalted butter
3/4 cup finely chopped onion
1/2 cup finely chopped celery
2 garlic cloves, minced
7 cups chicken broth
2 cups plain yellow cornmeal
1/2 tsp. salt
1/2 tsp. black pepper
3 tbs. finely chopped fresh sage
1/2 cup freshly grated Parmesan cheese

In a large sauce pan over medium heat, add 1/4 cup butter, onion, celery and garlic. Saute the vegetables for 4 minutes or until tender. Add the chicken broth and bring the broth to a boil. When the broth is boiling, slowly stir in the cornmeal. Stir in the salt, black pepper and sage. Stir frequently and reduce the heat to low. Simmer the polenta for 10 minutes.

Remove the pan from the heat and stir in the Parmesan cheese. Spray a 9 x 13 baking pan with non stick cooking spray. Pour the polenta into the baking pan. Cover the dish with plastic wrap and refrigerate the polenta at least 6 hours but up to 12 hours. When the polenta is firm, cut the polenta into 12 triangles.

In a large skillet over medium heat, add 1 tablespoon butter. When the butter melts, add 3 triangles. Cook about 3 minutes on each side or until golden brown. Remove the polenta from the skillet and keep warm. Prepare the rest of the polenta triangles adding the remaining butter as needed to fry the remaining polenta. Serve hot.

Basic Polenta with Variations

Makes about 3 1/2 cups

3 1/2 cups water or whole milk
3/4 tsp. salt
1 cup plain yellow cornmeal
Unsalted butter as needed

You can substitute 1 3/4 cups chicken broth and 1 1/4 cups water for 3 1/2 cups water and the salt if desired.

Add the water and salt to a sauce pan over medium heat. When the water comes to a boil, stir in the cornmeal. Stir constantly with a whisk. Reduce the heat to low and simmer the polenta about 10 minutes or until the polenta is thick and creamy. Line a loaf pan with plastic wrap. Spoon the polenta into the loaf pan. Cover the pan with plastic wrap and chill for 8 hours. When the polenta is chilled, remove the polenta from the pan using the plastic wrap as handles. Slice the polenta into slices. Pan fry or bake the slices until crisp on the outside and warm inside.

You can spoon the polenta into a plastic wrap lined shallow baking pan. Refrigerate for 8 hours. You can cut the polenta into squares or use cookie cutters for special designs.

To pan fry the polenta, add 2 tablespoons unsalted butter to a skillet over medium heat. When the butter melts, add slices of the polenta. Do not over crowd the skillet. Fry the polenta until crisp on both sides. Add additional butter if needed to fry the remaining slices.

To bake polenta slices, preheat the oven to 425°. Spray a baking sheet with non stick cooking spray. Place the slices on the baking sheet. Bake for 7-8 minutes or until lightly browned and hot.

Sausage and Peppers with Polenta: In a skillet over medium heat, add 8 oz. sliced Italian sausage. Cook for 5 minutes. Stir in 1 sliced red bell pepper, 1 sliced green bell pepper, 1 sliced onion, 14 oz. can Italian diced tomatoes and 1/2 teaspoon dried Italian seasoning. Saute for 5-6 minutes or until the sausage is well browned and no longer pink. Remove the skillet from the heat and drain off the excess grease. Spoon the sausage and peppers over cooked polenta slices. Sprinkle with grated Parmesan cheese if desired.

Tomato, Basil & Cheese Polenta: Set the oven to the broiler position. Place sliced Roma tomatoes and fresh basil over cooked polenta slices. Broil for 3 minutes. Place mozzarella cheese slices over the top and broil for 2 minutes or until the cheese is melted and bubbly.

Poached Eggs & Cheese Polenta: Place poached eggs and shredded cheddar cheese over hot cooked polenta slices. Broil for 1 minute if desired to melt the cheese.

Garlic Mushroom Polenta: In a skillet over medium heat, add 2 tablespoons unsalted butter. When the butter melts, add 8 oz. fresh sliced mushrooms and 2 garlic cloves. Saute for 5 minutes or until the mushrooms are tender. Spoon the mushrooms and garlic over hot cooked polenta slices. Sprinkle with grated Parmesan cheese if desired.

Basic Polenta with Variations cont'd

Garlic Polenta: Saute 2 minced garlic cloves in 2 tablespoons unsalted butter. Saute the garlic for 2 minutes. Add the garlic and butter along with 2 tablespoons whipping cream to the cornmeal while cooking. Follow the directions above to finish cooking the polenta.

Parsley Pecan Polenta: Add 1/2 cup chopped toasted pecans and 1/4 cup minced fresh parsley to the polenta while cooking. Follow the directions above to finish cooking the polenta.

Mozzarella Polenta: Stir 1/2 cup shredded mozzarella cheese into the polenta when removed from the heat. Stir until the cheese is melted. You can substitute your favorite cheese for the mozzarella if desired.

Sage, Rosemary or Italian Herb Polenta: Stir 1 1/2 teaspoons dried sage, rosemary or Italian seasoning into the polenta while cooking. Follow the directions above to finish cooking the polenta.

Mexican Shrimp & Grits

Makes 4 servings

10 oz. can diced tomatoes with lime and cilantro
1/4 cup heavy whipping cream
6 tbs. unsalted butter
3/4 cup quick cooking grits
4 slices bacon
1 lb. chorizo sausage, casing removed
1 onion, chopped
2 tbs. olive oil
8 oz. fresh shrimp, peeled and deveined
Tabasco sauce to taste
2 tbs. minced fresh cilantro
3/4 cup shredded Mexican cheese blend

Add the tomatoes and heavy cream to a large measuring cup. Add water if needed to make 3 cups. Pour the tomatoes into a sauce pan over medium heat. Stir in 2 tablespoons butter and bring to a boil. When the mixture boils, stir in the grits. Reduce the heat to low and stir constantly until the grits are thick and creamy. This takes about 5-6 minutes on my stove. Remove the pan from the heat and place a lid on the pan. Set aside for the moment.

In a large skillet over medium heat, add the bacon. Cook for 5-7 minutes or until the bacon is crispy. Remove the bacon from the pan and set aside for the moment. Drain off the bacon drippings.

Add the chorizo sausage and onion to the skillet. Stir frequently to break the sausage into crumbles as it cooks. Cook about 6 minutes or until the sausage is well browned and no longer pink. Remove the sausage and onion from the pan. Drain off the pan drippings.

In a separate skillet over medium heat, add the olive oil. When the oil is hot, add the shrimp. Pour a few drops Tabasco sauce over the shrimp if desired. Cook about 4 minutes or until the shrimp turn pink. Remove the pan from the heat and add 4 tablespoons butter. Let the butter melt over the shrimp.

In a serving dish, add the grits, bacon and sausage. Stir until combined. Spoon the shrimp and butter over the grits. Sprinkle the cilantro and Mexican cheese over the top. Serve with Tabasco sauce if desired.

Parmesan Shrimp Chorizo Grits

Makes 6 servings

3 cups water
3 cups vegetable or chicken broth
3/4 cup uncooked regular grits
1/4 cup unsalted butter
1/2 lb. shrimp, peeled, cooked, deveined and chopped
2 oz. chorizo sausage, chopped and cooked
4 oz. freshly grated Parmesan cheese
Salt and black pepper to season

In a large sauce pan over medium heat, add the water and vegetable broth. Bring the broth to a boil and stir in the grits. Reduce the heat to low and place a lid on the pan. Stir occasionally and simmer the grits about 15 minutes or until they are tender. Stir in the butter, shrimp, chorizo and Parmesan cheese. Season to taste with salt and black pepper. Remove the pan from the heat. Spoon the grits onto a serving platter or bowl.

Serve with sauteed onions and bell peppers or salsa over the top if desired.

Spoon Bread Grits with Mushroom Sauce

Makes 6 servings

2 3/4 cups chicken broth
1/2 cup quick cooking grits
1/4 cup plus 2 tbs. unsalted butter
1 cup whole milk
1 cup buttermilk
3 eggs, beaten
1 cup plain yellow cornmeal
1 tsp. baking powder
1 1/2 tsp. salt
1/4 tsp. baking soda
1/8 tsp. cayenne pepper
10 oz. shitake mushrooms, sliced
1 garlic clove, minced
2 tbs. all purpose flour
1/4 cup dry white wine
1/4 tsp. black pepper

In a large sauce pan over medium heat, add 1 3/4 cups chicken broth. Bring the broth to a boil and stir in the grits. Reduce the heat to low and simmer about 6 minutes or until the grits thicken. Stir frequently to keep the grits creamy. Remove the pan from the heat. Stir in 1/4 cup butter, milk, buttermilk and eggs. Whisk quickly to keep the eggs from cooking.

Stir in the cornmeal, baking powder, 1 teaspoon salt, baking soda and cayenne pepper. Preheat the oven to 425°. Spray a 11 x 7 baking dish with non stick cooking spray. Spoon the grits into the baking dish. Bake for 45 minutes or until the spoon bread is set and lightly browned. Remove the dish from the oven.

While the spoon bread is cooking, make the sauce. In a large skillet over medium heat, add 2 tablespoons butter. When the butter melts, add the mushrooms and garlic. Stir frequently and cook for 6 minutes or until the mushrooms are tender. Using a slotted spoon, remove the mushrooms and garlic from the skillet. Leave the pan drippings in the skillet.

Add the all purpose flour to the pan drippings. Whisk constantly and cook for 1 minute. Continue whisking and slowly add 1 cup chicken broth, white wine, 1/2 teaspoon salt and black pepper. When the sauce is combined, add the mushrooms back to the skillet. Stir constantly and cook until well combined and the sauce begins to thicken. Remove the skillet from the heat.

Cut the spoon bread into squares. Place the squares on a serving platter and spoon the mushroom sauce over the squares.

Grits Casserole

Makes 6 servings

4 1/2 cups water
1 tsp. salt
1 cup regular grits
2 eggs
3/4 cup whole milk
1/2 cup unsalted butter
2 cups garlic flavored cheese (or substitute your favorite cheese)

In a sauce pan over medium low heat, add the water and salt. Bring the water to a boil. Add the grits and stir for 2 minutes. Reduce the heat to low and simmer for 25-35 minutes or until the water is absorbed and the grits are tender. Stir frequently to keep the grits from sticking and burning. Remove the grits from the heat.

Preheat the oven to 350°. In a mixing bowl, add the eggs and milk. Whisk until well combined. Add the butter, cheese and grits. Stir until combined and the butter melts. Spray a 2 quart casserole dish with non stick cooking spray. Spoon the grits into the casserole dish. Bake for 30-40 minutes or until the casserole is set in the center. Remove the dish from the oven and serve.

Jalapeño Cheese Grits

Makes 8 servings

4 cups chicken broth
1 3/4 cups quick cooking grits
1/2 cup unsalted butter
1 onion, chopped
2 jalapeño peppers, seeded & diced
1 red bell pepper
2 garlic cloves, minced
2 cups shredded sharp cheddar cheese
2 cups shredded Monterey Jack cheese
5 eggs, beaten
1/4 tsp. salt

In a large sauce pan over medium heat, add the chicken broth. When the broth is boiling, stir in the grits. Stir frequently and simmer for 5 minutes or until the grits are tender. Remove the grits from the heat and place a lid on the pan.

In a large skillet over medium heat, add the butter. When the butter melts, add the onion, jalapeño peppers, red bell pepper and garlic. Saute for 5 minutes. Stir in the grits, cheddar cheese, Monterey Jack cheese, eggs and salt. Whisk until well combined and remove the skillet from the heat. Preheat the oven to 350°. Spray a 9 x 13 baking pan with non stick cooking spray. Pour the grits into the baking dish. Bake for 45 minutes or until the grits are set. Remove the dish from the oven and serve.

Smooth Cream Cheese Grits

Makes 6 servings

1 quart half and half
1/2 tsp. salt
1/4 tsp. garlic powder
1/4 tsp. black pepper
1 cup quick cooking grits
4 oz. cream cheese, cubed
1 1/2 cups shredded cheddar cheese
1/2 tsp. Tabasco sauce

In a large sauce pan over medium heat, add the half and half, salt, garlic powder and black pepper. Bring to a boil and slowly stir in the grits. Bring the grits back to a boil and reduce the heat to low. Stir occasionally and cook for 5 minutes. Add the cream cheese, cheddar cheese and Tabasco sauce to the grits. Stir until well combined and cook until the grits are tender, creamy and the cheeses melted. Remove the pan from the heat and serve.

Swiss and Cheddar Baked Grits

Makes 8 servings

4 1/3 cups water
3/4 tsp. salt
1 1/4 cups quick cooking grits
1/4 cup unsalted butter
1 1/2 cups shredded cheddar cheese
1/4 tsp. black pepper
3 eggs, beaten
1 1/4 cups shredded Swiss cheese

In a large sauce pan over medium heat, add the water and 1/2 teaspoon salt. Bring the water to a boil and stir in the grits. Stir frequently and reduce the heat to low. Place a lid on the pan and simmer about 5 minutes or until the grits are tender. Remove the pan from the heat. Stir in the butter, 1 cup cheddar cheese, 1/4 teaspoon salt and black pepper. Stir until the butter and cheese melt. Let the grits cool for 15 minutes.

Preheat the oven to 350°. Spray a 12 x 8 baking dish with non stick cooking spray. Stir the eggs into the grits. Spread half of the grits in the pan. Sprinkle the Swiss cheese over the grits. Spread the remaining grits over the cheese. Cover the dish with aluminum foil or a lid. Bake for 45-55 minutes or until the grits are set. Remove the aluminum foil and sprinkle 1/2 cup cheddar cheese over the top of the grits. Bake for 5 minutes. Remove the grits from the oven and serve.

Asiago Cheese Grits

Makes 6 servings

3 cups water
3 cups whole milk
1 tsp. salt
1 1/2 cups quick cooking grits
2 cups shredded Asiago cheese
1/3 cup chopped fresh basil
1/3 cup chopped fresh chives
1/3 cup chopped fresh parsley
3 tbs. unsalted butter
Additional salt and black pepper to taste

In a sauce pan over medium heat, add the water, milk and salt. Bring the liquids to a boil and slowly stir in the grits. Stir constantly and cook for 6 minutes or until the grits are thickened and tender. Remove the pan from the heat. Stir in the Asiago cheese, basil, chives, parsley and butter. Stir until the butter and cheese melt. Season to taste with salt and black pepper.

Smoked Gouda Grits

Makes 6 servings

4 cups water
4 cups whole milk
1 tsp. salt
1/2 tsp. black pepper
2 cups quick cooking grits
1 2/3 cups shredded Gouda cheese
3 tbs. unsalted butter

In a sauce pan over medium heat, add the water, milk, black pepper and salt. Bring the liquids to a boil and slowly stir in the grits. Stir constantly and cook for 5 minutes or until the grits are thickened and tender. Remove the pan from the heat and stir in the Gouda cheese and butter. Stir until the butter and cheese melt. Season to taste with additional salt and black pepper.

Bacon & Ham Grits Casserole

Makes a 9 x 13 baking dish

8 oz. bacon slices
8 oz. chopped cooked ham
1 1/4 cups whole milk
2 cups water
1 tsp. salt
3/4 cup quick cooking grits
1/4 cup unsalted butter
1 lb. Velveeta cheese, cubed
6 eggs, beaten
2 tsp. baking powder
1/2 tsp. black pepper

In a skillet over medium heat, add the bacon slices. Cook for 10 minutes or until the bacon is crisp. Remove the bacon from the skillet and drain on paper towels. Crumble the bacon. Remove all but 1 tablespoon of the bacon drippings from the skillet. Add the ham to the bacon drippings. Stir frequently and cook the ham about 5 minutes or until the ham is browned. Remove the ham from the skillet and set aside.

In a sauce pan over medium heat, add 3/4 cup milk, water and salt. Bring the water to a boil and slowly stir in the grits. Stir frequently and cook about 10 minutes or until the grits are tender and thick. Remove the pan from the heat and stir in the butter and Velveeta cheese. Stir until the cheese and butter melt. Stir in the bacon, ham, eggs, 1/2 cup milk, baking powder and black pepper.

Preheat the oven to 350°. Spray a 9 x 13 baking pan with non stick cooking spray. Spoon the grits into the baking dish. Bake for 45 minutes or until the casserole is set. Remove the dish from the oven and cool for 5 minutes before serving.

Mushroom Ragout with Grits

Makes 4 servings

2 cups fresh sliced mushrooms
1/4 cup olive oil
1/4 cup finely chopped shallots
3 cups chicken broth
2 tbs. chopped fresh parsley
2 tbs. chopped fresh chervil
6 tbs. softened unsalted butter
1 1/4 tsp. salt
1/4 tsp. black pepper
4 cups whole milk
1 cup regular white grits, uncooked
1 cup whipping cream

In a large skillet over medium heat, add the mushrooms and olive oil. Stir constantly and cook for 2 minutes. Add the shallots and cook for 1 minute. Continue stirring and slowly add the chicken broth. Bring the broth to a boil. Increase the heat to high and cook about 20 minutes or until the broth reduces and thickens. Stir in the parsley, chervil, 3 tablespoons butter, 1/4 teaspoon salt and 1/8 teaspoon black pepper. Remove the skillet from the heat.

About 15 minutes before the broth is ready, add the milk, 1 teaspoon salt and 1/8 teaspoon black pepper to a sauce pan over medium heat. Bring the milk to a boil and stir in the grits. Stir frequently and cook about 10 minutes or until the grits are tender. Slowly whisk in the whipping cream. Once the whipping cream is combined, add 3 tablespoons butter. Stir constantly until the butter melts. Remove the pan from the heat. Spoon the grits onto a platter and spoon the mushroom sauce over the grits.

Gumbo Grits Appetizer Bites

Makes a 15 x 10 x 1 jelly roll pan

2 cups chicken broth
1 cup whole milk
1 cup regular grits
4 tbs. unsalted butter
1/2 cup finely chopped andouille sausage
2 tsp. Creole seasoning
1/2 cup finely diced green bell pepper
1/3 cup finely diced red onion
2 garlic cloves, minced
8 okra pods, trimmed and cut into 36 slices
36 medium size raw shrimp, peeled and deveined

Preheat the oven to 350°. In a sauce pan over medium heat, add the chicken broth and milk. Bring the liquids to a boil and whisk in the grits. Continue whisking until the grits begin to boil. Reduce the heat to low and simmer for 10 minutes or until the grits are thick. Stir occasionally to keep the grits from sticking. Remove the pan from the heat.

In a skillet over medium heat, add 3 tablespoons butter. When the butter melts, add the andouille sausage. Saute for 5 minutes or until the sausage is hot and browned. Remove the skillet from the heat and stir the sausage into the grits.

Spray a 15 x 10 x 1 jelly roll pan with non stick cooking spray. Spread the grits in the pan. Bake for 25 minutes or until the grits are firm and lightly browned. Remove the grits from the oven and cool for 20 minutes.

In a skillet over medium heat, add 1 tablespoon butter, Creole seasoning, green bell pepper, red onion, garlic, okra and shrimp. Saute about 5 minutes or until the shrimp turn pink and are tender. Remove the skillet from the heat. Spoon the shrimp and vegetables over the grits. Cut into small pieces and serve.

Corn Jalapeño Grits Fritters

Makes about 22 fritters

2 cups whole milk
1 cup quick cooking yellow grits
3 tbs. unsalted butter, softened
1 tsp. baking powder
1 tsp. salt
2 eggs, beaten
1/4 cup chopped red bell pepper
1/2 cup finely chopped green onions
2 tsp. minced jalapeño pepper, seeded
2 tbs. finely chopped basil
1 cup fresh corn, cut from the cob
1/4 cup all purpose flour
3 tbs. olive oil

In a small bowl, add 1/2 cup milk and the grits. Let the grits sit for 3 minutes. In a large sauce pan over medium heat, add 1 1/2 cups milk. Bring the milk to a boil and slowly whisk in the grits. Stir constantly and cook for 2 minutes or until the grits are thickened. Remove the pan from the heat. Stir in the butter, baking powder, salt, eggs, red bell pepper, green onions, jalapeño pepper, basil, corn and all purpose flour. Stir until well combined.

You will need to cook the fritters in batches. In a large skillet over medium heat, add 1 tablespoon olive oil. When the oil is hot, drop the fritters by tablespoonfuls into the hot oil. Cook the fritters until the tops are covered with bubbles and the edges cooked. Flip the fritters over and cook about 2 minutes on the other side or until golden brown. Remove the fritters from the skillet and drain on paper towels if desired. Repeat with the remaining olive oil until all the fritters are cooked.

Bacon Grits Fritters

Makes about 30 fritters

4 cups whole milk
1 tsp. salt
1 cup quick cooking grits
1 1/2 cups extra sharp cheddar cheese, shredded
1/2 cup cooked finely crumbled bacon
2 green onions, minced
1/2 tsp. black pepper
2 eggs
1/4 cup water
3 cups panko breadcrumbs
Vegetable oil for frying

In a large sauce pan over medium heat, add the milk and salt. Bring the milk to a boil and slowly whisk in the grits. Whisk constantly and cook about 6 minutes or until the grits are tender. Remove the pan from the heat. Stir in the cheddar cheese, bacon, green onions and black pepper. Stir until well combined. Let the grits sit for 5 minutes. Spray an 8" square baking pan with non stick cooking spray. Spoon the grits into the pan. Cover the pan with plastic wrap. Refrigerate at least 4 hours but no longer than 24 hours.

Beat the eggs and water together in a small bowl. Place the breadcrumbs in a shallow dish. Form the grits into 1 1/2" balls using a heaping tablespoon of the grits. You will need to fry the fritters in batches. If you add too many fritters to the oil at one time, the temperature of the oil will drop and the fritters will be greasy and under cooked In a deep heavy skillet over medium high heat, add vegetable oil to a 3" depth. The temperature of the oil should be 350° when ready. While the oil is heating, dip the grits balls into the egg wash and then roll the balls in the bread crumbs. Drop the balls into the hot oil. Fry about 3 minutes per side or until the fritters are golden brown. Remove the fritters from the oil and drain on paper towels.

Southwestern Grits Cakes

Makes 4 servings

4 cups water
1 tsp. salt
1 cup quick cooking grits
1/2 cup chopped green onions
4 oz. can diced green chiles, drained
2 tbs. diced red pimento
1/8 tsp. Tabasco sauce
3 tbs. unsalted butter, softened
15 oz. can black beans, drained and rinsed
1 cup picante sauce
1 tomato, seeded and chopped
2 tbs. chopped fresh cilantro

In a sauce pan over medium heat, add the water and salt. Bring the water to a boil and stir in the grits. Stir constantly and bring the grits to a boil. Place a lid on the pan and reduce the heat to low. Simmer the grits for 5 minutes. Remove the pan from the heat and stir in the green onions, green chiles, red pimento and Tabasco sauce.

Grease a 9" square pan with 1 tablespoon butter. Pour the grits into the pan. Cover the pan with plastic wrap and refrigerate the grits until firm. The grits need to chill at least 3 hours. When the grits are firm, turn the grits out onto your work surface. Cut the grits into 4 squares. Cut each square into a triangle.

In a skillet over medium heat, add 2 tablespoons butter. When the butter melts, add the grits triangles. Fry the triangles about 5 minutes on each side or until golden brown and firm. Remove the grits from the skillet and place on a serving plate.

In a sauce pan over medium heat, add the black beans and picante sauce. Stir constantly and cook until the beans are boiling. Remove the pan from the heat and spoon over the grits. Sprinkle the tomatoes and cilantro over the top before serving.

Shrimp Stew & Grits

Makes 10 servings

1 1/2 cups chopped celery
3/4 cup chopped green bell pepper
1 cup chopped onion
2 tbs. unsalted butter, melted
3 lbs. small shrimp, peeled and deveined
2 tbs. cornstarch
3 tbs. Worcestershire sauce
1 tsp. salt
1/2 tsp. black pepper
1 tsp. seafood seasoning
1 cup water
1 cup chopped radishes
5 cups hot cooked grits

In a large skillet over medium heat, add the celery, green bell pepper, onion and butter. Saute about 5 minutes or until the vegetables are tender. Add the shrimp, cornstarch, Worcestershire sauce, salt, black pepper, seafood seasoning and water. Stir frequently and cook about 7-8 minutes or until the shrimp turn pink and are tender. Drain off the excess liquid.

Stir in the radishes. Cook only until the radishes are heated. Remove the skillet from the heat and spoon the grits onto a large platter. Spoon the shrimp over the grits and serve.

Baked Grits Stuffing

Makes 12 servings

3 cups water
1 1/2 tsp. salt
1/4 tsp. cayenne pepper
1/2 cup unsalted butter
1 cup uncooked regular grits
1 lb. smoked oysters, drained
1/2 cup freshly grated Parmesan cheese
1 red bell pepper, diced
8 green onions, chopped
3 eggs, beaten
1 cup fine dry breadcrumbs

In a sauce pan over medium heat, add the water, salt, cayenne pepper and butter. Bring the water to a boil and slowly stir in the grits. Stir constantly and bring the grits back to a boil. Place a lid on the pan and reduce the heat to low. Stir frequently and simmer the grits about 10 minutes or until tender and the liquid absorbed. Remove the grits from the heat and cool completely at room temperature.

Preheat the oven to 325°. Spray a 3 quart casserole dish or 9 x 13 baking dish with non stick cooking spray. Stir the oysters, Parmesan cheese, red bell pepper, green onions, eggs and breadcrumbs into the grits. Spoon the grits into the prepared baking dish. Bake for 40-45 minutes or until the stuffing is set and lightly browned. A knife inserted off center of the stuffing will come out clean when ready. Remove the dish from the oven and serve.

This is delicious with ham or duck.

Grits and Ham Pie

Makes a 9" pie

1 cup water
1/2 cup quick cooking grits
1 cup evaporated milk
3/4 cup shredded cheddar cheese
3/4 cup diced cooked ham
3 eggs, beaten
1 tbs. fresh minced parsley
1/2 tsp. dry mustard
1/2 tsp. Tabasco sauce
1/4 tsp. salt

In a sauce pan over medium heat, add the water. Bring the water to a boil and stir in the grits. Stir constantly and cook about 5 minutes or until the grits thicken. Remove the pan from the heat and stir in the evaporated milk, cheddar cheese, ham, eggs, parsley, dry mustard, Tabasco sauce and salt.

Preheat the oven to 350°. Spray a 9" pie pan with non stick cooking spray. Spoon the grits the pie pan. Bake for 30 minutes or until the grits are set and golden brown. Remove the pie from the oven and cool for 5 minutes before serving.

You can sprinkle finely chopped green onions over the top of the pie before serving if desired. This is an excellent brunch or breakfast pie. Serve with yogurt, fresh fruit and maple syrup if desired.

Grits Fiesta Pie

Makes 6 servings

1 1/2 cups water
1/4 tsp. garlic powder
1/2 cup quick cooking grits
1/4 cup all purpose flour
1/2 cup shredded cheddar cheese
3 eggs, beaten
3/4 lb. lean ground beef
1 pkg. taco seasoning mix
1 cup shredded Monterey Jack cheese
1/3 cup chopped tomato
1/4 cup sliced black olives
3 tbs. chopped green bell pepper
2 tbs. whole milk

In a large sauce pan over medium heat, add the water and garlic powder. Bring the water to a boil and slowly stir in the grits. Bring the grits back to a boil. Reduce the heat to low and cook for 4 minutes. Stir the grits occasionally while cooking. Remove the pan from the heat.

In a small bowl, stir together the all purpose flour and cheddar cheese. Add to the grits and stir until the cheese melts. Add 1 beaten egg to the grits. Stir until well combined. Spray a 9" pie pan with non stick cooking spray. Spoon the grits into the pie pan forming a pie crust. Press the grits into the pie pan with the back of a spoon. Set the crust aside for the moment.

In a skillet over medium heat, add the ground beef and taco seasoning mix. Stir frequently to break the ground beef into crumbles as it cooks. Cook about 6 minutes or until the ground beef is browned and no longer pink. Remove the skillet from the heat and spoon over the crust. Sprinkle 3/4 cup Monterey Jack cheese, tomato, black olives and green bell pepper over the top.

In a small bowl, whisk together 2 eggs and the milk. Pour the eggs over the pie. Preheat the oven to 375°. Bake for 25 minutes or until the pie is set and the crust lightly browned. Remove the pie from the oven and sprinkle 1/4 cup Monterey Jack cheese over the top. Let the pie rest for 5 minutes before slicing.

Pineapple Grits Pie

Makes two 9" pies

2 cups water
1/4 tsp. salt
1/2 cup uncooked quick cooking grits
8 oz. can crushed pineapple, drained
8 oz. pkg. cream cheese, softened
3 eggs
1 cup granulated sugar
1/2 cup whole milk
1/4 tsp. vanilla extract
2 graham cracker pie crust, 9" size

In a sauce pan over medium heat, add the water and salt. Bring the water to a boil and stir in the grits. Place a lid on the sauce pan and reduce the heat to low. Stir occasionally and simmer the grits about 5 minutes or until tender. Remove the pan from the heat. Preheat the oven to 300°. Pour the grits into a blender.

Add the pineapple and cream cheese to the blender. Process until smooth and well combined. Scrape down the sides of the blender if needed. With the blender running, slowly add the eggs. Add the eggs one at a time. Let the blender process each egg before adding the next egg. Add the granulated sugar, milk and vanilla extract. Process until well combined and pour into the graham cracker crust. Bake for 1 hour or until the pies are set in the center. Remove the pies from the oven and cool before serving.

Grillades and Grits

Makes 12 servings

4 lb. beef boneless rump roast
1/2 cup bacon drippings
1/2 cup all purpose flour
1 cup chopped onion
2 cups chopped green onions
3/4 cup chopped celery
1 1/2 cups chopped green bell pepper
2 garlic cloves, minced
2 cups peeled and chopped tomatoes
1/2 tsp. dried tarragon leaves
1 tsp. dried thyme
1 cup water
1 cup red wine
2 tsp. salt
1/2 tsp. black pepper
2 bay leaves
1/2 tsp. Tabasco sauce
2 tbs. Worcestershire sauce
3 tbs. fresh chopped parsley
8 cups boiling water
2 cups quick cooking grits
12 oz. jar process cheese spread

Trim excess fat if desired from the roast. Cut the roast into 1/2" slices. In a dutch oven, add 1/4 cup bacon drippings. When the drippings are hot, add the roast slices. Brown the slices about 2 minutes per side or until well browned. Remove the meat from the pot and set aside for the moment.

Add the remaining 1/4 cup bacon drippings to the dutch oven. When the drippings melt, stir in the all purpose flour. Stir constantly and cook until the roux is caramel colored. Stir in the onion, green onions, celery, green bell pepper and garlic. Stir constantly and cook about 5 minutes or until the vegetables are tender. Stir in the tomatoes, tarragon and thyme. Stir constantly for 3 minutes.

Add 1 cup water, red wine, 1 teaspoon salt, black pepper, bay leaves, Tabasco sauce and Worcestershire sauce to the pan. Stir until well blended. Add the roast slices to the pan and bring to a boil. Reduce the heat to low and place a lid on the pan. Simmer for 1 hour. Take the lid off the pan and simmer for 30 minutes. Remove the pan from the heat and remove the bay leaves. Stir in the parsley.

About 10 minutes before the roast is ready, make the grits. In a large sauce pan over medium heat, add 8 cups boiling water. Stir in the grits and 1 teaspoon salt. Stir constantly and reduce the heat to low. Simmer about 5 minutes or until the grits are tender. Add the processed cheese spread and stir until the cheese melts. Remove the pan from the heat and spoon the grits onto a serving platter.

Spoon the roast and sauce over the grits when ready to serve.

Sausage Grits

Makes 12-14 servings

1 lb. ground pork sausage
3 cups hot cooked grits
2 1/2 cups shredded cheddar cheese
3 tbs. unsalted butter
3 eggs, beaten
1 1/2 cups whole milk
2 tbs. minced fresh parsley
2 tbs. diced red pimento

In a skillet over medium heat, add the sausage. Stir frequently to break the sausage into crumbles as it cooks. Cook about 6-7 minutes or until the sausage is well browned and no longer pink. Remove the skillet from the heat and drain off the excess grease.

Preheat the oven to 350°. Spray a 9 x 13 casserole dish with non stick cooking spray. Spoon the sausage into the bottom of the casserole dish. In a mixing bowl, add the hot grits, cheddar cheese and butter. Stir until the cheese and butter melts and are well combined. Add the eggs and milk and stir until combined. Spread the grits over the sausage. Bake for 1 hour. Remove the dish from oven and sprinkle the parsley and red pimento over the top before serving.

Sausage & Cheddar Grits Casserole

Makes 8 servings

6 cups water
1 tsp. salt
1 1/2 cups quick cooking grits
1 lb. ground pork sausage
1 1/2 cups shredded sharp cheddar cheese
1 egg, beaten
2 tbs. picante sauce
1 tbs. dried minced onion

In a sauce pan over medium heat, add the water and salt. Bring the water to a boil and stir in the grits. Stir constantly and cook about 5 minutes or until the grits are tender. Remove the pan from the heat and keep the grits warm while you cook the sausage.

In a skillet over medium heat, add the pork sausage. Stir frequently to break the sausage into crumbles as it cooks. Cook about 6-7 minutes or until the sausage is well browned and no longer pink. Remove the skillet from the heat and drain off the grease.

Preheat the oven to 350°. Spray a 2 quart casserole dish with non stick cooking spray. Add the sausage, cheddar cheese, egg, picante sauce and onion to the grits. Stir until well combined. Spoon the grits into the prepared casserole dish. Bake for 30 minutes or until the casserole is set and lightly browned. Remove the casserole from the oven and cool for 5 minutes before serving.

Grits Italiano

Makes 8 servings

1 lb. hot ground pork sausage
1 1/2 lbs. lean ground beef
3 cups cooked grits
14 oz. jar pizza sauce
1/8 tsp. salt
1/8 tsp. black pepper
1/4 tsp. garlic powder
1 large green bell pepper, chopped
1 onion, chopped
2 1/2 cups shredded cheddar cheese

In a large skillet over medium heat, add the pork sausage and ground beef. Stir frequently to break the meat into crumbles as it cooks. Cook about 8-9 minutes or until the meats are well browned and no longer pink. Remove the skillet from the heat and pour off the excess grease.

Preheat the oven to 325°. Spray a 9 x 13 baking pan with non stick cooking spray. Spread the cooked grits into the bottom of the baking pan. In a small bowl, stir together the pizza sauce, salt, black pepper and garlic powder. Spoon half of the pizza sauce over the grits. Spoon half of the meat filling over the sauce. Sprinkle half the green bell pepper, onion and cheddar cheese over the meat.

Repeat the layering process one more time using the remaining pizza sauce, meat, green bell pepper, onion and omitting the cheddar cheese layer. Bake for 25 minutes. Sprinkle the cheddar cheese over the top. Bake for 10 minutes or until the cheese is melted and bubbly. Remove the pan from the oven and cool for 5 minutes before serving.

Baked Garlic Cheese Grits

Makes 8 servings

4 cups water
4 cups whole milk
1 1/4 tsp. salt
2 cups regular grits
2 containers garlic and herb spreadable cheese, 6 oz. size
1 cup shredded Parmesan cheese
1 tsp. black pepper
4 eggs, beaten
8 bacon slices, cooked and crumbled
3/4 cup chopped fresh parsley

I use Alouette or Boursin cheese spread in this dish. I have also used garlic and herb cream cheese.

In a large sauce pan over medium heat, add the water, milk and salt. Bring the liquids to a boil and stir in the grits. Bring the grits to a boil and reduce the heat to low. Stir frequently and simmer about 20 minutes or until the grits are tender. Stir in the garlic and herb cheese, Parmesan cheese and black pepper. Remove the pan from the heat. Add the beaten eggs to a mixing bowl. Add 1/4 cup hot grits to the eggs. Whisk quickly until combined and add to the grits in the pan. Stir until well mixed.

Preheat the oven to 350°. Spray a 9 x 13 baking dish with non stick cooking spray. Spoon the grits into the baking dish. Bake for 45-55 minutes or until the casserole is set in the center. Remove the dish from the oven and sprinkle the bacon and parsley over the top before serving.

Hot Tomato Grits

Makes 6 servings

2 slices bacon, chopped
3 1/2 cups chicken broth
1/2 tsp. salt
1 cup quick cooking grits
2 large ripe tomatoes, peeled and chopped
2 tbs. canned chopped green chiles
1 cup shredded cheddar cheese

In a large heavy sauce pan over medium heat, add the bacon. Cook about 5 minutes or until the bacon is crisp. Remove the bacon from the pan but leave the drippings in the pan. Drain the bacon on paper towels. Stir in the chicken broth and salt. Bring the broth to a boil and stir in the grits, tomatoes and green chiles. Stir frequently and bring the grits to a boil. Keep stirring and reduce the heat to low. Simmer the grits for 15-20 minutes or until tender, thick and creamy.

Remove the pan from the heat and stir in the cheddar cheese and bacon. Stir until the cheese melts. Let the grits sit for 5 minutes before serving.

Creamy Grits

Makes 4 servings

4 cups chicken broth
1/2 cup whipping cream
1 cup quick cooking grits
2 cups shredded cheddar cheese

In a large sauce pan over medium heat, add the chicken broth and whipping cream. Bring the liquids to a boil and stir in the grits. Stir constantly until the grits come back to a boil.

When the grits are boiling, reduce the heat to low and place a lid on the sauce pan. Simmer the grits for 5-6 minutes or until tender. Remove the pan from the heat and stir in the cheddar cheese. Stir until the cheese melts. Let the grits sit for 5 minutes before serving.

Ham & Spinach Grits

Makes a 11 x 7 baking pan

1 head garlic
3 tsp. olive oil
4 oz. thinly sliced ham, cut into 1/4" strips
1 tbs. vegetable oil
3 cups chicken broth
1 cup quick cooking grits
1/2 cup unsalted butter
1/4 tsp. salt
1/4 tsp. black pepper
1 cup whole milk
4 eggs
1 cup shredded Swiss cheese
10 oz. pkg. frozen chopped spinach, thawed and drained
1/4 cup grated Parmesan cheese

Cut the peaks off the garlic head just slightly exposing the garlic cloves. Place the garlic on a sheet of aluminum foil. Drizzle the olive oil over the top of the garlic. Wrap the aluminum foil around the garlic forming a packet. Preheat the oven to 350°. Place the foil packet on a baking sheet. Bake for 1 hour. The garlic should be soft when ready. Remove the garlic from the oven and let the garlic cool completely before using.

Squeeze the garlic from each clove into a food processor. Process until the garlic is smooth. Scrape down the sides of the food processor if needed. In a skillet over medium heat, add the ham and vegetable oil. Saute about 5 minutes or until the ham is well browned. Remove the ham from the skillet and drain on paper towels.

In a large sauce pan over medium heat, add the chicken broth. When the broth comes to a boil, stir in the grits. Stir frequently and cook the grits about 5 minutes or until they are tender. Remove the pan from the heat. Add the garlic, butter, salt, milk and black pepper to the grits. Stir until well combined. Add the eggs to the grits and whisk until well combined. Gently fold in the ham, Swiss cheese and spinach.

Preheat the oven to 350°. Spray a 11 x 7 baking dish with non stick cooking spray. Spoon the grits into the baking dish. Sprinkle the Parmesan cheese over the top of the dish. Bake for 35-45 minutes or until the dish is puffed and firm. Remove the grits from the oven and serve.

Grits Timbales

Makes 12 servings

6 cups water
2 1/2 tsp. salt
1 1/2 cups uncooked regular grits
2 garlic cloves, minced
1 1/2 cups shredded cheddar cheese
5 tbs. grated Parmesan cheese
1/2 tsp. black pepper
3 egg yolks, beaten
1/2 cup whipping cream
4 tbs. unsalted butter, softened
Boiling water

In a large sauce pan over medium heat, add 6 cups water and 2 teaspoons salt. Bring the water to a boil and stir in the grits. Stir constantly and cook for 2 minutes. Stir frequently and cook about 15 minutes or until the grits are tender. Stir in the garlic, cheddar cheese, 2 tablespoons Parmesan cheese, 1/2 teaspoon salt and black pepper. In a small bowl, stir together the egg yolks and whipping cream. Remove the grits from the heat. Add 1/4 cup grits to the egg yolks. Whisk until well combined. Add the egg yolks to the grits. Whisk until well combined.

Preheat the oven to 350°. Butter twelve 4 ounce ramekin cups with the softened butter. Spoon the grits into each ramekin. Place the ramekins in a large roasting pan. Pour boiling water to a depth of 1" up the side of the roasting pan. Cover the roasting pan with aluminum foil. Place the pan in the oven and bake about 30 minutes or until the grits are set.

Remove the pan from the oven. Remove the ramekins from the pan and place on a baking sheet. Sprinkle 3 tablespoons Parmesan cheese over the grits. Turn the oven to the broiler position. Place the baking sheet in the oven and broil for 2 minutes. Remove the pan from the oven. Let the grits cool for 2 minutes before serving.

Grits & Greens Dinner Bake

Makes 6 servings

4 cups water
1/2 tsp. salt
1 cup uncooked regular grits
10 oz. pkg. frozen spinach, thawed and well drained
2 cups shredded Swiss cheese
1 1/2 cups cooked chopped ham
2 eggs, beaten
1 tbs. yellow prepared mustard
1/2 cup grated Parmesan cheese

In a sauce pan over medium heat, add the water and salt. Bring the water to a boil and stir in the grits. Reduce the heat to low and place a lid on the pan. Simmer for 5 minutes. Stir in the spinach, Swiss cheese and ham. Stir constantly until the cheese melts. Remove the pan from the heat. Stir in the eggs and mustard. Preheat the oven to 325°. Spray an 8" square baking pan with non stick cooking spray.

Spoon the grits into the pan. Sprinkle the Parmesan cheese over the top. Bake for 40 minutes or until the grits are set and golden brown on top. A knife inserted in the center of the dish should come out clean when ready. Remove the casserole from the oven and serve.

Grits & Collard Greens

Makes 6 servings

1 lb. fresh collard greens
1 cup heavy whipping cream
4 cups chicken broth
1 cup stone ground grits
1/4 to 1/2 cup whole milk
1/4 cup unsalted butter
1 to 1 1/2 cups freshly grated Parmesan cheese
1/2 tsp. black pepper
1/2 cup cooked crisp bacon, crumbled, optional

Remove the stems from the greens. Wash the greens thoroughly and chop into bite size strips. In a large sauce pan over medium low heat, add the whipping cream and 3 cups chicken broth. Stir until well combined. Bring the broth to a boil and slowly stir in the grits. Bring the grits back to a boil. Stir frequently and place a lid on the pan. Cook for 15 minutes. Slowly add 1/4 cup whole milk to the grits. Stir constantly when adding the milk. Cook the grits about 10 minutes or until they are tender. If the grits are too thick, slowly whisk in the remaining 1/4 cup whole milk.

In a large skillet over medium heat, add 1 cup chicken broth and the collard greens. Bring the greens to a boil. Reduce the heat to low and place a lid on the skillet. Simmer for 5 minutes. Remove the skillet from the heat and drain all the liquid from the greens. I place the greens in a colander to drain. Pat the greens dry with paper towels. You need most of the moisture removed from the greens.

Stir the butter, 1 cup Parmesan cheese and black pepper into the hot grits. Add the remaining Parmesan cheese if desired. Stir the greens into the grits and sprinkle the bacon across the top if desired.

Baked Hominy Grits with Cheese

Makes 4 servings

2 cups water
2 cups whole milk
1 tsp. salt
1 cup hominy grits
2 eggs, beaten
1 cup shredded sharp cheddar cheese
2 tbs. plus 1 tsp. unsalted butter

You can use instant grits or regular grits. Cook instant grits about 5 minutes and regular grits about 20-30 minutes.

In a sauce pan over medium heat, add the water, milk, salt and hominy grits. Stir constantly and bring the grits to a boil. Reduce the heat to low and simmer until the grits are thickened. Add the eggs to a small bowl. Add 1/4 cup grits to the eggs and stir until well combined. Add the eggs to the sauce pan with the grits. Stir until well combined. Remove the pan from the heat and stir in the cheddar cheese.

Preheat the oven to 350°. Grease a 1 quart casserole dish with 1 teaspoon butter. Pour the grits in the casserole dish. Cut 2 tablespoons butter into pieces. Place the butter over the grits. Bake for 30-40 minutes or until the top is lightly browned. Remove the dish from the oven. Sprinkle the grits with crispy cooked bacon if desired.

Chicken and Grits

Makes 4 servings

3 1/2 cups chicken broth
1 cup quick cooking grits, uncooked
8 oz. jar process cheese spread (Cheez Whiz)
3 eggs, beaten
2 cups cooked chopped chicken
1/2 tsp. poultry seasoning
3 tbs. finely chopped green onions, optional

In a sauce pan over medium heat, add the chicken broth. When the broth is boiling, slowly stir in the grits. Stir for 2 minutes. Place a lid on the sauce pan and reduce the heat to low. Stir occasionally and cook for 3 minutes or until the grits are tender. Remove the pan from the heat. Stir in the cheese spread, eggs, chicken and poultry seasoning. Stir until well combined.

Preheat the oven to 375°. Spray a 11 x 7 baking dish with non stick cooking spray. Spoon the grits into the baking dish. Bake for 30 minutes. Remove the dish from the oven and sprinkle the green onions over the top if desired.

Cheesy Grits Poppers

Makes about 10 appetizer servings

1 cup hot cooked grits
1 cup shredded cheese (Pepper Jack, cheddar, Colby, etc.)
1/2 cup shredded Parmesan cheese
2 tbs. fresh minced cilantro
1 garlic clove, minced
20 sweet mini bell peppers

We like to use Pepper Jack cheese, but use whatever cheese you like. In a mixing bowl, add the grits, shredded cheese, Parmesan cheese, cilantro and garlic. Stir until well combined. Cover the bowl with plastic wrap and chill about 8 hours.

Split each bell pepper in half lengthwise. Leave the stems on the peppers. Use the stems to pick up each popper. Scoop out the seeds. Spoon the grits into each pepper half. Preheat the oven to the broiler position. Place the peppers on a baking sheet. Broil for 4-6 minutes or until the grits are hot, the peppers broiled and the cheese melted. Remove the pan from the oven and serve.

Grits Bread

Makes 1 loaf

2 tbs. vegetable oil
3 cups cooked grits
1 cup plain white or yellow cornmeal
1 tbs. baking powder
1/2 tsp. salt
4 eggs, beaten
1/2 cup unsalted butter, melted
1 cup cooked sausage or bacon, crumbled
1/4 to 1/2 cup whole milk

Preheat the oven to 400°. Grease a loaf pan with the vegetable oil. In a mixing bowl, add the grits, cornmeal, baking powder, salt, eggs, butter and sausage. Stir until well combined. Only add enough milk to make a batter the consistency of thick pancake batter.

Pour the batter into the prepared pan. Bake for 45-55 minutes or until a toothpick inserted in the center of the bread comes out clean. Remove the pan from the oven and let the bread cool for 15 minutes before removing the bread from the pan. This bread will be dense and resemble a firm spoon bread instead of a quick bread. It is delicious!

Quick Grits Souffle

Makes 8 servings

4 cups water
2 cups instant grits
2 cups whole milk
1 cup unsalted butter
4 eggs

In a sauce pan over medium low heat, add the water. When the water begins to boil, add the grits. Stir constantly for 2 minutes. Add the milk and butter. Stir until the butter melts. Reduce the heat to low and place a lid on the sauce pan. Cook for 10 minutes. Stir occasionally to keep the grits from sticking or burning. Remove the pan from the heat and cool the grits for 10 minutes.

Preheat the oven to 350°. Spray a 2 quart round casserole dish with non stick cooking spray. Add the eggs to the grits and whisk until well combined. Spoon the grits into the casserole dish. Bake for 30-35 minutes or until the grits are set and hot. Remove the dish from the oven and serve.

Cheddar Grits Souffle

Makes 12 servings

6 cups boiling water
1 1/2 cups regular grits
2 tsp. season salt
1 tsp. onion salt
1 tsp. garlic salt
3/4 tsp. Worcestershire sauce
1/2 cup plus 1 tbs. unsalted butter
3 eggs, beaten
4 cups cubed cheddar cheese
Paprika to taste

In a sauce pan over medium heat, add the boiling water. Make sure the water is boiling before adding the grits. Stir constantly and add the grits. Cook for 5 minutes. Add the season salt, onion salt, garlic salt, Worcestershire sauce and 1/2 cup butter. Stir until well combined and remove the grits from the heat. The grits will not be finished at this point.

Preheat the oven to 350°. Butter a 2 quart souffle dish with 1 tablespoon butter. In a small bowl, add the beaten eggs. Stir 2 tablespoons grits into the eggs. Whisk until well combined. Add the eggs to the grits in the pan and whisk until well combined. Stir in the cheddar cheese. Spoon the grits into the souffle dish. Sprinkle the paprika, if desired, over the top of the casserole.

Bake for 1 1/2 hours or until the grits are tender and the souffle fluffy. Remove the dish from the oven and serve immediately.

Puffy Cheese Grits

Makes a 9 x 13 baking dish

1 cup whole milk
1 tsp. salt
1 cup quick cooking grits
1/3 cup unsalted butter
1/4 tsp. black pepper
4 egg yolks
1 1/2 cups shredded Monterey Jack cheese
8 egg whites, at room temperature
1/4 tsp. cream of tartar

Preheat the oven to 425°. Spray a 9 x 13 baking pan with non stick cooking spray. In a sauce pan over medium heat, add the milk and salt. Bring the milk to a boil and stir in the grits. Reduce the heat to low. Stir constantly and simmer for 3-5 minutes or until the grits thicken. Remove the pan from the heat.

Stir in the butter and black pepper. Stir until the butter melts. Add the egg yolks, one at a time, to the grits. Whisk each egg yolk into the grits before adding the next egg yolk. Stir in the Monterey Jack cheese when all the egg yolks are combined.

In a mixing bowl, add the egg whites and cream of tartar. Using a mixer on medium speed, beat until the egg whites form stiff peaks. Fold 1/3 of the egg whites into the grits. Fold until combined. Gently fold in the remaining egg whites. Spoon the grits into the prepared baking dish. Bake for 20 minutes or until the grits are puffed and browned. Remove the dish from the oven and serve immediately as the dish will fall quickly.

Fried Grits

Makes 10 slices

5 cups water
1 tsp. salt
1 cup regular grits
3 tbs. bacon drippings or vegetable oil
Powdered sugar, optional
Maple syrup, optional

In a sauce pan over medium low heat, add the water and salt. Bring the water to a boil and add the grits. Stir constantly for 2 minutes. Stir frequently and cook for 20-30 minutes or until the grits are thick and tender. Reduce the heat to low if the water is evaporating too fast. Remove the pan from the heat.

Spray a loaf pan with non stick cooking spray. Pour the grits into the loaf pan. Refrigerate for 8 hours or overnight. When the grits are cold, turn the loaf pan out onto a platter. Slice the grits into slices about 3/4" thick.

In a skillet over medium low heat, add the vegetable oil or bacon drippings. When the oil begins to shimmer, add the slices. Cook about 2 minutes on each side or until browned and crispy. Remove the grits from the skillet and drain on paper towels. Sprinkle with powdered sugar or drizzle with maple syrup if desired.

Note: I serve these grits for dinner with creamed chicken poured over the top or slices of roast beef with gravy. You can also add crumbled cooked bacon to the grits before pouring the grits into the loaf pan.

Chicken Baked Grits Casserole

Makes 8 servings

3 cups cooked grits
2 cups cooked and diced chicken
2 cups cooked green peas
2 cans cream of chicken soup, 10.75 oz. size
1 1/2 cups shredded cheddar cheese

Preheat the oven to 350°. Spray a 3 quart casserole dish with non stick cooking spray. Add the grits, chicken, green peas, cream of chicken soup and 1 cup cheddar cheese to the dish. Stir until well combined.

Bake for 40-50 minutes or until the casserole is set. Sprinkle the remaining 1/2 cup cheddar cheese over the top of the casserole. Bake for 5 minutes. Remove the casserole from the oven and let the casserole rest for 10 minutes before serving.

Cheese Grits Souffle

Makes 6 servings

4 cups water
1 tsp. salt
1 cup instant grits
15 oz. jar Cheez Whiz
1/2 cup unsalted butter
4 eggs
Boiling water for baking

In a sauce pan over medium low heat, add the water and salt. When the water begins to boil, add the grits. Stir constantly for 2 minutes. Reduce the heat to low. Cover the sauce pan and cook for 6-8 minutes or until the grits are tender and most of the liquid is absorbed. Remove the grits from the heat and cool for 10 minutes.

Preheat the oven to 350°. Spray a 2 quart casserole dish with non stick cooking spray. Add the Cheez Whiz, butter and eggs to the grits. Stir until well combined and the butter melts. Spoon the grits into the casserole dish.

Place the casserole dish in a large baking pan. Pour boiling water to 1" up the sides of the casserole dish. Place the casserole and pan in the oven. Bake for 45-50 minutes or until the grits are set. Remove the dish from the oven and serve immediately.

Spicy Cheese Grits

Makes 6 servings

7 cups water
1 tsp. salt
1 1/2 cups regular grits
1 lb. sharp cheddar cheese, shredded
2 eggs
1 tbs. Worcestershire sauce
1 garlic clove, minced
1/2 cup unsalted butter
8 drops Tabasco sauce

In a sauce pan over medium low heat, add the water and salt. When the water begins to boil, add the grits. Stir constantly for 2 minutes. Reduce the heat to low. Cover the sauce pan and cook for 20-25 minutes or until the grits are tender and thick. Stir frequently to keep the grits from sticking and burning. Remove the grits from the heat and stir in 12 ounces cheddar cheese, eggs, Worcestershire sauce, garlic, butter and Tabasco sauce.

Preheat the oven to 350°. Spray a 3 quart casserole dish with non stick cooking spray. Spoon the grits into the casserole dish. Bake for 30 minutes. Sprinkle the remaining cheese across the top of the grits. Bake for 10-15 minutes or until the cheese melts and the casserole is set. Remove the dish from the oven and serve.

Garlic and Herb Cheese Grits

Makes 5 cups

4 cups chicken broth
1 cup quick cooking grits
5 oz. container garlic and herb spreadable cheese
1/4 tsp. black pepper

In a sauce pan over medium heat, add the chicken broth. When the broth comes to a boil, stir in the grits. Stir constantly and cook the grits about 6-7 minutes or until tender and thick. Remove the pan from the heat. Stir in the garlic and herb cheese and black pepper. Mix until well combined. Serve immediately.

You can substitute garlic and herb or garden vegetable cream cheese spread for the spreadable cheese if desired.

Country Grits & Sausage Casserole

Makes a 9 x 13 baking dish

2 lbs. ground pork sausage
4 cups water
1 1/4 cups quick cooking grits
4 cups shredded sharp cheddar cheese
1 cup whole milk
1/2 tsp. dried thyme
1/8 tsp. garlic powder
4 eggs, beaten
Paprika
1 tomato, cut into thin wedges

In a skillet over medium heat, add the pork sausage. Stir frequently to break the sausage into crumbles as it cooks. Cook about 10 minutes or until the sausage is browned and no longer pink. Remove the pan from the heat and drain off the excess grease.

In a large sauce pan over medium heat, add the water. When the water comes to a boil, stir in the grits. Stir frequently and cook the grits about 5 minutes or until they are tender. Remove the pan from the heat and stir in the cheddar cheese, milk, thyme and garlic powder. Stir until the cheese melts.

Stir the sausage and eggs into the grits. Stir quickly so the eggs do not scramble. Preheat the oven to 350°. Spray a 9 x 13 baking pan with non stick cooking spray. Pour the grits into the casserole dish. Sprinkle paprika to taste over the top of the grits. Bake for 1 hour or until the casserole is golden brown and hot. Remove the dish from the oven and cool for 5 minutes. Place the tomato wedges over the top before serving.

Mexican Grits Casserole

Makes 6 servings

3/4 cup white grits, uncooked
3 cups water
1 cup cream style corn
1 lb. ground beef
1 1/4 cups chopped onion
15 oz. can beef chili
1 tbs. chili powder
2 tsp. ground cumin
1/8 tsp. garlic salt
2 cups shredded cheddar cheese

In a sauce pan over medium low heat, add the water. When the water begins to boil, add the grits. Stir constantly for 2 minutes. Reduce the heat to low and add the cream style corn. Simmer for 15-18 minutes or until the grits are tender and most of the water is absorbed. Remove the grits from the heat.

In a skillet over medium low heat, add the ground beef and onion. Stir frequently to break the meat into crumbles as it cooks. Cook for 8 minutes or until the ground beef is well browned and no longer pink. Drain off the excess grease. Add the chili, chili powder, cumin and garlic salt. Stir until well combined. Stir frequently and simmer for 10 minutes. Remove the skillet from the heat.

Preheat the oven to 350°. Spray a 3 quart casserole dish with non stick cooking spray. Spoon the grits into the prepared casserole dish. Spoon the meat filling over the grits. Sprinkle the cheddar cheese over the top. Bake for 30-40 minutes or until the casserole is hot and the cheese melted. Remove the dish from the oven and serve.

This is delicious with salad and iced tea.

Baked Cheese and Garlic Grits

Makes 8 servings

4 cups water
1/2 tsp. salt
1 cup uncooked quick cooking grits
1 1/2 cups shredded cheddar cheese
1/2 cup unsalted butter
1/2 cup whole milk
1 garlic clove, minced
2 eggs, beaten

In a sauce pan over medium heat, add the water and salt. Bring the water to a boil and stir in the grits. Stir constantly until the grits begin to boil. Reduce the heat to low and simmer the grits about 20 minutes. Stir frequently while the grits are cooking for a creamy texture. When the grits thicken and are almost done, stir in the cheddar cheese, butter, milk and garlic. Stir constantly until the butter and cheese melt. Remove the pan from the heat.

Place the beaten eggs in a small bowl. Add about 1/4 cup grits to the eggs. Whisk until combined. Slowly add the eggs to the grits. Stir until combined. Preheat the oven to 325°. Spray a 2 quart casserole dish with non stick cooking spray. Spoon the grits into the casserole dish. Bake for 1 hour or until a toothpick inserted off center of the grits comes out clean. Remove the dish from the oven and serve.

Orange Grits

Makes 6 servings

12 bacon slices
3 cups water
1 tsp. salt
1 cup quick cooking grits
1/4 cup unsalted butter
1 tsp. grated orange zest
1 cup orange juice
4 eggs, beaten
2 tbs. light brown sugar

In a large skillet over medium heat, add the bacon. Cook about 7-8 minutes or until the bacon is crisp. Remove the bacon from the skillet and drain on paper towels.

In a sauce pan over medium heat, add the water and salt. Bring the water to a boil and stir in the grits. Stir constantly and cook for 4 minutes. Remove the pan from the heat. Add the butter, orange zest, orange juice and eggs. Stir until well combined.

Preheat the oven to 350°. Spray a 1 1/2 quart casserole dish with non stick cooking spray. Spoon the grits into the casserole dish. Sprinkle the brown sugar over the grits. Bake for 45 minutes or until a knife inserted in the center of the casserole comes out clean. Remove the dish from the oven and sprinkle the bacon over the top.

Sliced Cheese Grits

Makes 8 servings

1 cup quick cooking grits
1 quart whole milk
1/4 cup unsalted butter
1/2 tsp. salt
3 tbs. unsalted butter, melted
1 cup shredded Swiss cheese
1/3 cup freshly grated Parmesan cheese

In the top of a double boiler, add the grits, milk, 1/4 cup butter and salt. Stir frequently and cook about 20-30 minutes or until the grits thicken and are bubbly. Remove the pan from the heat. Spray a 9 x 13 baking dish with non stick cooking spray. Spoon the grits into the baking dish. Let the grits sit at room temperature until the grits are firm. When the grits are firm, slice the grits into 12 rectangular slices.

Preheat the oven to 400°. Place the grit slices in a 9" square baking pan. You will have to overlap the slices to make them fit. Drizzle the melted butter over the slices. Sprinkle the Swiss cheese and Parmesan cheese over the top of the slices. Bake for 25 minutes or until the cheeses melt and the slices are hot. Remove the pan from the oven and serve.

Nassau Grits

Makes 8 servings

8 bacon slices
1 onion, chopped
2 green bell peppers, finely chopped
15 oz. can diced tomatoes
1/4 tsp. granulated sugar
6 cups water
1 tsp. salt
1 1/2 cups uncooked regular grits

In a skillet over medium heat, add the bacon. Cook about 7 minutes or until the bacon is crisp. Remove the bacon from the skillet and drain on paper towels. Crumble the bacon into pieces. Drain all but 2 tablespoons bacon drippings from the skillet. Add the onion and green bell peppers to the skillet. Saute for 4 minutes. Stir in the tomatoes with juice and granulated sugar. Bring the vegetables to a boil. Reduce the heat to low and simmer for 30 minutes.

In a large sauce pan over medium heat, add the water and salt. Bring the water to a boil and stir in the grits. Stir frequently and cook for 15-20 minutes or until the grits are thick and tender. Remove the grits from the heat and stir in the tomato mixture. Spoon the grits into a serving dish. Sprinkle the bacon over the top and serve.

Baked Cheese Grits

Makes 6 servings

2 1/2 cups whole milk
3/4 cup uncooked regular grits
1/2 cup unsalted butter
1/2 tsp. salt
1/3 cup grated Parmesan cheese
5 oz. jar process sharp cheese spread

In a sauce pan over low heat, add the whole milk. Bring the milk to a boil and stir in the grits. Stir frequently and cook until the grits thicken. Stir in the butter, salt, Parmesan cheese and cheese spread. Remove the pan from the heat.

Preheat the oven to 325°. Spray a 1 quart casserole dish with non stick cooking spray. Spoon the grits into the casserole dish. Bake for 20 minutes or until the grits are tender and set. Remove the dish from the oven and serve.

Scrambled Grits

Makes 4 servings

2 tbs. bacon drippings
2 1/2 cups cold cooked grits
2 eggs, beaten

In a 10" heavy skillet over medium heat, add the bacon drippings. While the bacon drippings melt, add the grits to a mixing bowl. Using a fork, break up the grits. Add the eggs and whisk until combined.

Spoon the grits and eggs into the hot bacon drippings. Spread the grits over the bottom of the skillet. Cook for 2-3 minutes or until the bottom of the grits are well browned on the bottom. Using a fork, whisk the grits until they are the consistency of scrambled eggs. This will only take a few minutes to cook the grits. Remove the skillet from the heat. Serve with maple syrup if desired.

Gruyere Cheese Grits

Makes 8 servings

1 quart whole milk
1/2 cup unsalted butter
1 1/2 cups shredded Gruyere cheese
1 cup uncooked regular grits
1 tsp. salt
1/8 tsp. black pepper
1/3 cup grated Parmesan cheese

In a large heavy sauce pan over medium heat, add the milk. When the milk begins to boil, stir in 1/4 cup butter and Gruyere cheese. Stir constantly until the cheese melts. When the cheese melts, slowly stir in the grits. Add the salt and black pepper to the grits. Stir until combined. Remove the pan from the heat. Using a mixer on medium speed, beat the grits for 5 minutes.

Preheat the oven to 400°. Spray an 8" square pan with non stick cooking spray. Spoon the grits into the pan. In a small sauce pan over low heat, add 1/4 cup butter and the Parmesan cheese. Stir constantly until the cheese melts. Remove the pan from the heat and spread over the top of the grits. Bake for 30 minutes or until the grits are creamy and firm. Remove the grits from the oven and serve immediately.

Surprise Coconut Cream Pie

Makes a 9" pie

2 1/2 cups water
1/2 cup regular grits
1 cup granulated sugar
2 tbs. unsalted butter
2 eggs, beaten
1 1/2 cups sweetened flaked coconut
1/2 cup sour cream
9" prepared chocolate graham cracker crust
Sweetened whipped cream

In a sauce pan over medium heat, add the water. Bring the water to a boil and stir in the grits. Reduce the heat to low and place a lid on the pan. Stir the grits occasionally and cook for 15 minutes. Remove the pan from the heat and whisk in the granulated sugar and butter. Whisk until the butter and sugar melt. Add the eggs to a small bowl. Add 1/4 cup grits to the eggs. Whisk until combined and add to the grits. Stir until well blended.

Place the pan back over low heat. Stir constantly and cook until the temperature reaches 160° on a candy thermometer. Remove the pan from the heat and stir in the coconut and sour cream. Spoon the pie filling into the graham cracker crust. Cover the pie loosely with plastic wrap and refrigerate until the pie is well chilled. Spread sweetened whipped cream over the pie before serving.

Grits Pudding

Makes 4 servings

1 cup water
1/4 tsp. salt
1/4 cup quick cooking grits
2 cups whole milk
1 tbs. unsalted butter
2 eggs
1/4 cup granulated sugar
1/3 cup raisins
1/8 tsp. ground cinnamon, optional
Boiling water

In a sauce pan over medium heat, add the water and salt. When the water boils, stir in the grits. Stir frequently and cook for 5 minutes or until the grits are tender. Slowly stir in the whole milk. Bring the grits back to a boil and stir in the butter. Remove the pan from the heat. In a small bowl, add the eggs. Whisk the eggs until foamy and combined. Add 1/4 cup grits to the eggs and whisk until well combined. Add the eggs to the grits and stir until well combined. Stir in the granulated sugar, raisins and cinnamon.

Preheat the oven to 350°. Spray a 1 1/2 quart baking dish with non stick cooking spray. Spoon the grits into the baking dish. Place the baking dish in a roasting pan. Pour boiling water to a 1" depth on the baking dish. Bake for 1 hour. Stir the pudding every 20 minutes. Remove the pudding from the oven and let the pudding sit for 5 minutes before serving.

Mexican Hominy

Makes 4 servings

1/2 cup chopped onion
1 garlic clove, minced
1 tbs. vegetable oil
15 oz. can yellow hominy, drained
1 cup chopped tomato
2 tbs. chopped green chiles
1/2 tsp. chili powder
1/8 tsp. salt
1/4 tsp. black pepper
1/2 cup shredded sharp cheddar cheese

In a skillet over medium heat, add the onion, garlic and vegetable oil. Saute for 4 minutes. Stir in the hominy, tomato, green chiles, chili powder, salt and black pepper. Stir until combined and remove the skillet from the heat.

Preheat the oven to 350°. Spray a 1 quart baking dish with non stick cooking spray. Spoon the hominy into the baking dish. Bake for 25 minutes or until the dish is hot and bubbly. Sprinkle the cheddar cheese over the top. Bake for 5 minutes. Remove the dish from the oven and serve.

Chile Hominy Bake

Makes 4 servings

1 lb. ground beef
1/2 cup chopped onion
2 tbs. all purpose flour
1 tsp. salt
1 tsp. chili powder
15 oz. can hominy
15 oz. can diced tomatoes
1/4 cup shredded cheddar cheese

In a skillet over medium heat, add the ground beef and onion. Stir frequently to break the ground beef into crumbles as it cooks. Cook about 6-7 minutes or until the ground beef is browned and no longer pink. Drain off the excess grease. Stir in the all purpose flour, salt, chili powder, hominy with liquid and tomatoes with liquid. Stir until well combined and remove the skillet from the heat.

Preheat the oven to 350°. Spray a 2 quart casserole dish with non stick cooking spray. Spoon the filling into the baking dish. Bake for 25 minutes. Sprinkle the cheddar cheese over the top. Bake for 5 minutes or until the cheese melts and the dish is bubbly. Remove the dish from the oven and serve.

Hominy Ole'

Makes 6 servings

2 cans drained golden hominy, 15 oz. size
12 oz. jar salsa
3 cups shredded sharp cheddar cheese
1/4 tsp. black pepper

Preheat the oven to 350°. Spray an 8" square baking dish with non stick cooking spray. Add all the ingredients to the baking dish. Stir until combined and spread the hominy out in the dish. Bake for 30 minutes or until the dish is hot and cheese melts. Remove the dish from the oven and serve.

Hominy Sausage Bake

Makes 6 servings

1 lb. ground pork sausage
3/4 cup chopped onion
3/4 cup chopped celery
16 oz. can tomato sauce
1/4 tsp. dried oregano
15 oz. can golden hominy, drained
2 cups shredded Monterey Jack cheese

In a skillet over medium heat, add the sausage, onion and celery. Stir frequently to break the sausage into crumbles as it cooks. Cook about 6 minutes or until the sausage is well browned and no longer pink. Drain off the excess grease. Pat the sausage in the skillet with paper towels to remove as much grease as you can. Stir in the tomato sauce and oregano. Reduce the heat to low and simmer for 5 minutes. Remove the skillet from the heat.

Preheat the oven to 350°. Spray a 2 quart baking dish with non stick cooking spray. Spread half of the hominy in the bottom of the casserole dish. Spoon half of the sausage filling over the hominy. Sprinkle 1 cup Monterey Jack cheese over the sausage. Spread the remaining hominy over the cheese. Spoon the remaining sausage over the hominy. Bake for 20 minutes or until the dish is hot and bubbly. Sprinkle 1 cup Monterey Jack cheese over the top of the dish. Bake for 5 minutes. Remove the dish from the oven and serve.

Hominy Bean Salad

Makes 8 servings

15 oz. can yellow hominy, drained
16 oz. can red kidney beans, drained
1/4 cup sliced green onions
1/3 cup diced cucumber
1/4 cup diced red bell pepper
2 tbs. minced fresh parsley
3 tbs. vegetable oil
1/4 cup plus 1 tbs. cider vinegar
1 tbs. water
1/2 tsp. dried Italian seasoning
1 tsp. spicy brown mustard
1/8 tsp. celery seeds
1/4 tsp. chili powder
1/4 tsp. Tabasco sauce
1 cup alfalfa sprouts

In a mixing bowl, add the hominy, kidney beans, green onions, cucumber, red bell pepper and parsley. Toss until combined. In a mixing bowl, add the vegetable oil, cider vinegar, water, Italian seasoning, brown mustard, celery seeds, chili powder and Tabasco sauce. Whisk until well combined. Pour the dressing over the hominy and beans. Toss until all the ingredients are coated in the dressing. Cover the bowl with a lid or plastic wrap. Refrigerate for 8 hours.

When ready to serve, remove the vegetables and beans from the bowl using a slotted spoon. Place the vegetables and beans in a serving bowl. Sprinkle the alfalfa sprouts over the top before serving. You can pour the dressing left in the bowl over the alfalfa sprouts if desired.

Bean and Hominy Soup

Makes 12 cups

I love this soup using pantry ingredients. It is quick to make and provides a hearty meal in less than an hour.

3 cans great northern beans, 15 oz. size
15 oz. can hominy
14 oz. can stewed tomatoes
11 oz. can condensed bean with bacon soup
10 oz. can diced tomatoes and green chiles
15 oz. can whole kernel corn
2 cups water
2 bay leaves
1 tbs. dried cilantro
1 tsp. ground cumin
1 cup shredded sharp cheddar cheese

In a large sauce pan over medium heat, add the great northern beans with liquid, hominy with liquid, tomatoes with liquid, bean and bacon soup, tomatoes and green chiles with liquid, corn with liquid, water, bay leaves, cilantro and cumin. Stir until well combined. Bring the soup to a boil. Once the soup is boiling, reduce the heat to low and place a lid on the pan. Simmer for 30 minutes and remove the pan from the heat. Remove the bay leaf and discard. Spoon the soup into bowls and sprinkle the cheddar cheese over the top of each serving.

Southwest Hominy Soup

Makes 4 servings

1/3 cup chopped green bell pepper
1/4 cup chopped onion
1 tbs. vegetable oil
10 oz. can condensed tomato soup
1 1/4 cups chicken broth
1 1/3 cups water
4 oz. can diced green chiles, drained
15 oz. can golden hominy, drained

In a large sauce pan over medium heat, add the green bell pepper, onion and vegetable oil. Saute for 5 minutes. Stir in the tomato soup, chicken broth, water, green chiles and hominy. Stir occasionally and simmer the soup for 10 minutes. Remove the soup from the heat and serve.

Pork & Sausage Chile Hominy

Makes 6 servings

2 onions, chopped
2 garlic cloves, minced
2 tbs. vegetable oil
4 cups chicken broth
1 lb. lean boneless pork, cut into 1/2" cubes
3 dried red chiles, seeded and chopped
1 tsp. dried oregano
1/2 tsp. black pepper
1/4 lb. hot Italian sausage, diced
15 oz. can white hominy, drained

In a large sauce pan or dutch oven, add the onions, garlic and vegetable oil. Saute for 3 minutes. Add the chicken broth, pork, red chiles, oregano and black pepper. Stir until well combined. Bring to a boil and reduce the heat to low. Place a lid on the pot and simmer for 2 hours or until the pork is tender.

In a skillet over medium heat, add the Italian sausage. Saute for 5 minutes or until the sausage is well browned and no longer pink. Drain the grease from the sausage. Stir in the hominy and cook for 2 minutes. Remove the skillet from the heat and add to the pot with the pork. Stir until well combined. Remove the pot from the heat and serve.

Hot Cheese Hominy

Makes 8 servings

1/4 cup chopped onion
2 tbs. unsalted butter
2 cans drained golden or white hominy, 15 oz. size
8 oz. can diced green chiles, drained
1 cup sour cream
1 tsp. chili powder
1/4 tsp. salt
1/8 tsp. black pepper
1 1/2 cups shredded cheddar cheese

In a skillet over medium heat, add the onion and butter. Saute for 4 minutes. Add the hominy, green chiles, sour cream, chili powder, salt, black pepper and 1/2 cup cheddar cheese. Stir until well combined. Remove the skillet from the heat.

Preheat the oven to 400°. Spray a 2 quart casserole dish with non stick cooking spray. Pour the hominy into the casserole dish. Bake for 20 minutes. Sprinkle 1 cup cheddar cheese over the top of the casserole. Bake for 5 minutes. Remove the dish from the oven and serve.

Hominy Chili Casserole

Makes 4 servings

15 oz. can chili with beans
1/3 cup sliced black olives
1/2 cup onion, finely chopped
15 oz. can golden hominy, drained
1 cup shredded sharp cheddar cheese

Preheat the oven to 350°. Spray a 1 1/2 quart casserole dish with non stick cooking spray. Add the chili and half of the black olives to the casserole dish. Stir until combined. Sprinkle the onion over the top. Spread the hominy over the top of the dish. Bake for 25 minutes or until the dish is hot and bubbly. Sprinkle the cheddar cheese and remaining black olives over the top. Bake for 5 minutes. Remove the dish from the oven and serve.

CHAPTER INDEX

Cornmeal

Serrano Chile Blue Cornbread, 2
Southern Cornbread, 3
Carrot Cornbread, 3
Sour Cream Cornbread, 4
Honey Cornbread, 4
Pecan Cornbread, 5
Spiced Pecan Cornbread, 6
Herbed Cornbread, 7
Ultimate Cornbread, 8
Picante Cornbread, 9
Cottage Cheese Cornbread, 9
Custard Cornbread, 10
Wampus Bread, 11
Molasses Johnnycake, 11
Southwestern Cornbread Cakes, 12
Frankfurter Cornmeal Patties, 13
Corn Fritters, 14
Cowboy Cornbread, 15
Cheesy Beef Cornbread, 16
Gouda Cornbread, 17
Hot Water Cornbread with Variations, 18
Sour Cream Cornmeal Muffins, 19
Apple Corn Muffins, 20
Everyday Cornmeal Muffins, 20
Bisquick Cornbread Muffins, 21
Broccoli Cornbread Muffins, 21
Tomato Corn Muffins, 22
Parmesan Corn Muffins, 23
Spicy Cornbread Muffins, 24
Sour Cream & Corn Cornbread Muffins, 25
Cornmeal Yeast Muffins, 26
Cheesy Cornbread Muffins, 27
Corn Oat Muffins, 28
Tex Mex Corn Muffins, 29
Corn Husk Sunflower Corn Muffins, 30
Blue Corn Muffins, 31
Southern Cracklin' Cornbread, 32
Paprika Cornbread, 33
Buttermilk Corn Sticks, 34
Angel Corn Sticks, 35
Fresh Corn Cornbread, 36
Cheddar Cornbread, 37

Cornmeal cont'd

Honey Cornbread, 38
Savory Cornbread, 39
Mexican Cornbread, 40
Garlic Thyme Cornbread, 41
Hot Mexican Cornbread, 42
Spinach Cornbread, 43
Pecan Cornmeal Rounds, 44
Corn Dogs, 45
Corn Dog Bites, 46
Cornbread Croutons, 47
Cheese Cornmeal Croutons, 48
Cornmeal Pastry, 49
Cornmeal Waffles, 50
Cheddar Pecan Cornmeal Waffles, 51
Corn Chile Waffles, 52
Blue Cornmeal Blueberry Pancakes, 53
Cornmeal Dumplings, 54
Blue Corn Crepes, 55
Mexican Cornbread Salad, 56
Old Fashioned Hush Puppies, 57
Mexican Hush Puppies, 58
Bacon Hush Puppies, 59
Tomato Onion Hush Puppies, 60
Fiery Beer Hush Puppies, 61
Corn Hush Puppies, 62
Mississippi Hush Puppies, 63
Squash Puppies, 64
Acorn Squash Puppies, 65
Shrimp Puppies, 66
Baked Hush Puppies, 67
Green Onion Tomato Hush Puppies, 68
Peppery Hush Puppies, 69
Aunt Jenny's Hush Puppies, 70
Onion Cornbread Shortcake, 71
Green Onion Hoecakes, 72
Lacy Corn Cakes, 72
Southern Corn Cakes, 73
Hearty Cornmeal Pancakes, 73
Spinach Cornbread Bake, 74
Garlic Spoon Bread, 74
Mushroom Spoon Bread, 75
Corn and Bacon Spoon Bread, 76
Old Fashioned Southern Spoon Bread, 77
Cheese Spoon Bread, 78
Cornbread Vegetable Supper, 79

Cornbread Stuffed Peppers, 80
Tamale Meatballs, 81
Cornbread Tamale Pie, 82
Easy Creamed Chicken over Cornbread, 83
Sausage Cornbread Dressing, 84
Green Chile Cornbread Dressing, 85
Granny's Cornbread Dressing, 86
Squash Cornbread Dressing, 87
Kentucky Cornbread Dressing, 88
Old Fashioned Cornbread Dressing, 89
Oyster Cornbread Dressing, 90

Grits

Polenta with Sausage, 92
Grilled Polenta with Black Bean Salsa, 93
Baked Okra & Cheese Polenta, 94
Skillet Polenta Squares, 95
Sage Pan Fried Polenta, 96
Basic Polenta with Variations, 97
Mexican Shrimp & Grits, 99
Parmesan Shrimp Chorizo Grits, 100
Spoon Bread Grits with Mushroom Sauce, 101
Grits Casserole, 102
Jalapeño Cheese Grits, 103
Smooth Cream Cheese Grits, 104
Swiss and Cheddar Baked Grits, 104
Asiago Cheese Grits, 105
Smoked Gouda Grits, 105
Bacon & Ham Grits Casserole, 106
Mushroom Ragout with Grits, 107
Gumbo Grits Appetizer Bites, 108
Corn Jalapeño Grits Fritters, 109
Bacon Grits Fritters, 110
Southwestern Grits Cakes, 111
Shrimp Stew & Grits, 112
Baked Grits Stuffing, 113
Grits and Ham Pie, 114
Grits Fiesta Pie, 115
Pineapple Grits Pie, 116
Grillades and Grits, 117
Sausage Grits, 118
Sausage & Cheddar Grits Casserole, 119
Grits Italiano, 120
Baked Garlic Cheese Grits, 121
Hot Tomato Grits, 122
Creamy Grits, 122
Ham & Spinach Grits, 123
Grits Timbales, 124
Grits & Greens Dinner Bake, 125
Grits & Collard Greens, 126
Baked Hominy Grits with Cheese, 127
Chicken and Grits, 128
Cheesy Grits Poppers, 128
Grits Bread, 129
Quick Grits Souffle, 129
Cheddar Grits Souffle, 130
Puffy Cheese Grits, 131
Fried Grits, 132

Chicken Baked Grits Casserole, 133
Cheese Grits Souffle, 133
Spicy Cheese Grits, 134
Garlic and Herb Cheese Grits, 134
Country Grits & Sausage Casserole, 135
Mexican Grits Casserole, 136
Baked Cheese and Garlic Grits, 137
Orange Grits, 138
Sliced Cheese Grits, 139
Nassau Grits, 139
Baked Cheese Grits, 140
Scrambled Grits, 140
Gruyere Cheese Grits, 141
Surprise Coconut Cream Pie, 142
Grits Pudding, 143
Mexican Hominy, 144
Chile Hominy Bake, 145
Hominy Ole', 145
Hominy Sausage Bake, 146
Hominy Bean Salad, 147
Bean and Hominy Soup, 148
Southwest Hominy Soup, 148
Pork & Sausage Chile Hominy, 149
Hot Cheese Hominy, 150
Hominy Chili Casserole, 150

ABOUT THE AUTHOR

Lifelong southerner who lives in Bowling Green, KY. Priorities in life are God, family and pets. I love to cook, garden and feed most any stray animal that walks into my yard. I love old cookbooks and cookie jars. Huge NBA fan who loves to spend hours watching basketball games. Enjoy cooking for family and friends and hosting parties and reunions. Can't wait each year to build gingerbread houses for the kids.

Printed in Great Britain
by Amazon